Penguin Modern Poets

VOLUME 9

John Burnside was born in Fife, Scotland. He has published five collections of poetry, including *The Myth of the Twin* (Jonathan Cape, 1994), which was selected for the New Generation Poets and shortlisted for the T. S. Eliot Prize, and *Swimming in the Flood* (Jonathan Cape, 1995). In 1994 he received the Geoffrey Faber Memorial Award. He is currently working on a novel, *The Dumb House*, which is to be published in early 1997, and on a new collection of poetry.

Robert Crawford was born in Bellshill, near Glasgow, in 1959. His collections of poetry include *A Scottish Assembly* (Chatto, 1990), *Talkies* (Chatto, 1992), *Masculinity* (Cape, 1996) and *Sharawaggi* (co-authored with W. N. Herbert; Polygon, 1990). His critical books include *The Savage and the City in the Work of T. S. Eliot* (OUP, 1987), *Devolving English Literature* (OUP, 1992) and *Identifying Poets: Self and Territory in Twentieth-Century Poetry* (Edinburgh University Press, 1993), as well as various edited volumes. He is editing *The Democratic Voice: Poetry Since 1945 from Britain and Ireland* with Simon Armitage, to be published by Viking and Penguin. He lives in St Andrews, Fife, and is Professor of Modern Scottish Literature at the University of St Andrews.

Kathleen Jamie was born in 1962. She studied Philosophy at Edinburgh University, and began writing in her teens. As well as her poetry, she has published a travel book about northern Pakistan, entitled *The Golden Peak* (Virago, 1992). Her poetry has won several awards, including a Somerset Maugham Award in 1995 and the Geoffrey Faber Memorial Award in 1996. She lives in Fife with her husband and son.

The Penguin Modern Poets Series

Volume One
James Fenton
Blake Morrison
Kit Wright

Volume Two
Carol Ann Duffy
Vicki Feaver
Eavan Boland

Volume Three
Glyn Maxwell
Mick Imlah
Peter Reading

Volume Four
Liz Lochhead
Roger McGough
Sharon Olds

Volume Five
Simon Armitage
Sean O'Brien
Tony Harrison

Volume Six
U. A. Fanthorpe
Elma Mitchell
Charles Causley

Volume Seven
Donald Davie
Samuel Menashe
Allen Curnow

Volume Eight
Jackie Kay
Merle Collins
Grace Nichols

Volume Nine
John Burnside
Robert Crawford
Kathleen Jamie

Volume Ten
Douglas Oliver
Denise Riley
Iain Sinclair

Penguin Modern Poets

VOLUME 9

JOHN BURNSIDE

ROBERT CRAWFORD

KATHLEEN JAMIE

PENGUIN BOOKS

Published by the Penguin Group
Penguin Books Ltd, 27 Wrights Lane, London W8 5TZ, England
Penguin Books USA Inc., 375 Hudson Street, New York, New York 10014, USA
Penguin Books Australia Ltd, Ringwood, Victoria, Australia
Penguin Books Canada Ltd, 10 Alcorn Avenue, Toronto, Ontario, Canada M4V 3B2
Penguin Books (NZ) Ltd, 182–190 Wairau Road, Auckland 10, New Zealand

Penguin Books Ltd, Registered Offices: Harmondsworth, Middlesex, England

This selection first published 1996
10 9 8 7 6 5 4 3 2 1

Set in 10.5/14 pt Monotype Garamond
Typeset by Datix International Limited, Bungay, Suffolk
Printed in England by Clays Ltd, St Ives plc

Contents

John Burnside

Ukiyo-e

Puddles of *mirin* and soy
on our crusted plates,

daikon, *matsuba*,
a half-eaten muscle of eel,

and those plums in their bitter juice
at the rim of your bowl,

as if we had met in Kyoto
or ghostly Nagoya

and climbed here out of the snow
through a lake of bamboo.

The drum bridge at Kameido almost appears
when I open the curtains,

then drizzle, and London Road,
and the old

hospital, locked in its acre
of knotweed and pines:

those smudges of black on the leaves
like a printmaker's ink,

drying for two hundred years,
while we almost recover

the smoke of Minami,
the vinegar hidden in thaw.

A normal skin

The wet days come like a rash:
after a month of sun, the windowpanes
are clouded with the afterlife
of cat fur and busy-lizzies,
and, gloved in her latest attack
of eczema, our silent neighbour
sits between her curtains like a burning
candle, her face turned aside,
her shoulders hunched.
She's taking apart the clocks she collected all year
at boot fairs and local fêtes
and laying them out in pieces on the table.
She knows how things are made – that's not the point –
what matters is the order she creates
and fixes in her mind:
a map of cogs and springs, laid out in rows,
invisibly numbered.
What we desire in pain
is order, the impression of a life
that cannot be destroyed, only dismantled.
For years you would buy those razors with orange handles,
the toothpastes and mild shampoos for a sensitive skin
I never had. For years, I took apart
the memories I thought would make me whole
being unravelled.
What we desire in pain
is reason: an impression of ourselves
as wounded, explained,
coerced from a destination.

Late at night,
our neighbour draws her curtains, disappears,
and lies in the healing darkness, half-awake,
achieving a normal skin
by an effort of will.

I'm not the one you thought
was sensitive, the soul you hoped to find:
arriving home, still wet with moonlit rain,
I enter the silence you left, in a dreamless house,
and reckon how little I feel,
when I stop to listen.

Halloween

I have peeled the bark from the tree
to smell its ghost,
and walked the boundaries of ice and bone
where the parish returns to itself
in a flurry of snow;

I have learned to observe the winters:
the apples that fall for days
in abandoned yards,
the fernwork of ice and water
sealing me up with the dead
in misted rooms

as I come to define my place:
barn owls hunting in pairs along the hedge,
the smell of frost on the linen, the smell of leaves
and the whiteness that breeds in the flaked
leaf mould, like the first elusive threads
of unmade souls.

The village is over there, in a pool of bells,
and beyond that nothing,
or only the other versions of myself,
familiar and strange, and swaddled in their time
as I am, standing out beneath the moon
or stooping to a clutch of twigs and straw
to breathe a little life into the fire.

Avoirdupois

The weight of mercury and frost,
or the plover's weight of remorse
at the root of my tongue

when I stood in the polished hall
and my grandfather died by ounces
a door's-breadth away.

No one could measure his house:
the loads were too subtle, too fine:
the weight of hooks, the swish of gaberdine,

his ghosts come in to tea, still damp with rain,
stains in the books Aunt Eleanor had read
the year she died,

and where he lay, the weight of riverbeds:
the tide of shadows under Fulford burn
where fat trout swam like phantoms in the weeds

and where I saw him once, big and alive,
dabbling his hands in the water, as if he would lift
the fish of our dreams, the catch that would break the scales.

The myth of the twin

Someone is still awake
in the night of my grandfather's house
with its curtains and potted palms
and its books full of beech leaves
pressed so the colours would stay,

and someone is having the dream
I had for weeks: out walking on the beach
I lifted a pebble and split it
open, like an apricot, to find
a live child hatched in the stone;

like radio, the whisper of the tide,
the feel of a pulse in the dark, when I stay up all night
and answers come, single and clear, like the calling of birds,
or the pull of the sea, when the moon sails high in the clouds
and I pick out the shapes on its surface: a handprint, an iris.

Swimming in the flood

Later he must have watched
the newsreel,

his village erased by water: farmsteads and churches
breaking and floating away

as if by design;
bloated cattle, lumber, bales of straw,

turning in local whirlpools; the camera
panning across the surface, finding the odd

rooftop or skeletal tree,
or homing in to focus on a child's

shock-headed doll.
Under it all, his house would be standing intact,

the roses and lime trees, the windows,
the baby grand.

He saw it through the water when he dreamed
and, waking at night, he remembered the rescue boat,

the chickens at the prow, his neighbour's pig,
the woman beside him, clutching a silver frame,

her face dislodged, reduced to a puzzle of bone
and atmosphere, the tremors on her skin

wayward and dark, like shadows crossing a field
of clouded grain.

Later, he would see her on the screen,
trying to smile, as they lifted her on to the dock,

and he'd notice the frame again, baroque and absurd,
and empty, like the faces of the drowned.

Dundee

The streets are waiting for a snow
that never falls:
too close to the water,
too muffled in the afterwarmth of jute,
the houses on Roseangle
opt for miraculous frosts
and the feeling of space that comes
in the gleam of day
when you step outside for the milk
or the morning post
and it seems as if a closeness in the mind
had opened and flowered:
the corners sudden and tender, the light immense,
the one who stands here proven after all.

A swimming lesson

Maybe it's luck, or a talent for going naked
that lets one body mingle with the stream
till fingers and eyes and even the lungs
are water. Maybe it's a gift
for transformation,
changing from child to swan at the river's edge,
from swan to fish, from fish to waterweed.
And maybe it's a pledge to gravity
that keeps another wedded to the earth,
the way I would dive to prove the riverbed
before I could swim midstream,
probing the mud with my fingers, clawing up handfuls
of pebbles and silt, and drowned bodies
eased from their bones
– I had to know that solid ground was there,
while she was drifting, merging with the tide,
taking a form from the water and making it hers,
accepting its favours, repaying the debt in kind.

In my dream you are sitting out
at the edge of the water,
watching me wade towards you in the dark:
time has stood still since the river
leached out the last thread of warmth and left you to dry,
the blue of your lips, the strawberry-red of your mouth,
a lure for the boys who found you, a lifetime away.
In my dream I am lifting the eyes from your milky skull
and I'm placing these pebbles of glass in the empty sockets
to see if they'll quicken and heal in your salvaged flesh.

She lived at the far end of town.
After the lesson, she'd leave me and wander away
through coal-black woods beyond the railway yards
where men and dogs were hunting in the grass,
drawing their secret kills from a web of static.
I never went that far, I always stopped,
though sometimes I thought I was there, in my scarf and
gloves,
standing out under an elm tree, watching the shadows
flare from my torch beam, up in the higher boughs.
There were houses out there, there were rooms filled with
spiders and damp
where children could go for a dare and be unreturned,
– empty blouses, sandals, cotton socks –
and ten yards into the bushes, a holy well
that was only a puddle of mud and clouded rain,
where Ellen MacInnes was brushed by a sand-coloured wing
and wandered home pregnant.

Waiting for you to step
like a heron out of the slow
green river,
I watched the reed beds
darken with a long caressing wind,
and wondered what we leave
beneath the silt,
footprints and tangles of hair
that will sink forever,
that bracelet you once let fall
through the streaming weeds
– diving for almost an hour, we came up
empty-handed, feeling it settle and drift,

like the bodies we shed
when we hoist ourselves on to the bank,
moving away for good
in a skin's depth of water.

She swam in the dark and the light,
but midnight was what she knew
like the warp of her mind,
the cattle gathered round to watch her rise,
the smell of the trees, the leaf-melt that clung to her fingers
– so it was dawn when they found her
somewhere downriver,
a nakedness for everyone to share,
boys on the footpath,
policemen with hooks and lines
– and I'd choose to remember
a country of mile-deep woods,
shoals of fishes hanging in the streams
like coloured flags, and my shadow swimming away
on a field of barley,
but all I can see is the mud in the lines of her face,
and the scatter of leaves
that someone has brushed aside,
revealing the clouded skin, and the gas-blue eyes
where thinking has stopped,
like the calm at the edge of a snowfall.

Summer

When the heat fades
the dog-fox returns,
tracing an earlier path along the lane,
a glimmer of self
in the mazework of blood and urine.
The pine trees are still.
From village to village you hear
the same dull murmur of bees
and the shiver that quickens the hedge
is only the wind,

but tonight we could almost believe
in fairies: how they surface through the grass
or drift through the kitchen,
stitching our milk with venom,
tonight they are almost here, though nothing is here
but the day's warmth, fading away
through brickwork and skin
and the rice-paper ghost of the moon on an open field
where the barn owl descends
to a parish of barley and nettles.

from PAROUSIA

IV

It was less of a stream than a border:
a rill over wheat-coloured stones, then a sudden
dimming.
                And that was the place to cross,
treading the cold, my bare feet snagging a depth
of fish-skin and weed,
that was the kingdom of pike, where the body was laid
a finger's-depth under the sand.

The far side was stranger's country, a half-mile away:
a back road far in the heat, a gust of wind,
cow parsley, mare's tails, a glimmer of slate in the distance,
and out in the open field, a dog-fox
pausing in its stride, to scent the air,
the only spirit I could understand
the black awareness rooted in its eyes.

A heresy, but soul becomes
conceivable, immersed in viscera,
and mind endures, in wisps of meat and bone;
at twilight, crossing the river, I always knew
something was close, but all I ever saw
was blood-warm, vivid, wholly physical:
the sparrow-hawk sweeping the air, the questing owl,
the stoat in the wall, that knows where its hunger is going.

The Light Institute

I was an extra, walking home alone
in a matinée rain,

vaguely aware of the church, and the hunting owls
on Stenhouse Street, the house-of-horror bats

circling the lamps, a sub-fluorescent dust
of popcorn and velour, sprinkled on my clothes

like spots of light.
Mother was Myrna Loy
in the empty kitchen,

standing at the centre of the world
with flour on her hands, in a halo of musk and steam,

and someone else was coming from the gold
of infinite distance, someone I would know

from memory: the master of the house,
plugged into the undertow of scripts

where I could happen, suddenly alive,
chosen for something, leaving my bed in the dark

and crossing the yard to meet him on the far
border of knowledge and skill,

the hero now, the one I should have been:
Walter Pidgeon. Gable. Franchot Tone.

Septuagesima

Nombres.
Están sobre la pátina
de las cosas.
Jorge Guillén

I dream of the silence
the day before Adam came
to name the animals,

the gold skins newly dropped
from God's bright fingers, still
implicit with the light.

A day like this, perhaps:
a winter whiteness
haunting the creation,

as we are sometimes
haunted by the space
we fill, or by the forms

we might have known
before the names,
beyond the gloss of things.

Home Movie

They are one generation away
from Gaelic, or Latin,
walking the orchards in spray suits and surgical masks,
their science-fiction bodies catch the light
or thicken and set in the shadows, like evening dew,

and I am the one who has come
from the distant city,
stumbling upon their magic, their ram's heads and candles,
the singing at midnight, the dance on the moonlit green,
their stubborn games
of death and resurrection.

I should have left the village reels ago:
as soon as I met the children on the cliffs
I should have guessed – that laughter in the grass,
their knowing looks, the whispers in their sleeves.
I should have listened when the doctor spoke,
clumsy and fearful, barring the surgery door,
and when his body washed up on the rocks
covered with stings and bruises, I should have known.

Now I am packing my bags in an upstairs room
while, somewhere below, the solstice is set to begin.
I still intend to take the next train out
– as soon as the midwife comes, in her starched white dress
to give me her blessing: an apple; a copper nail;
a name from the churchyard;
the dead in their cradles of drowning.

Love Poem

To think in the old language;
to waken at dawn
on the borders of dunlin and tern

with the same words, day after day,
remnants of healing and song
informing our house,

our only work, to keep in mind
the recipes and marginalia
of other times, the lore of clouds and tides,

or simply, when we come in from the dark,
to name things for the beauty of the sounds:
uisge; *aran*; *oidhche*; *gealach*; *teine*.

Epistemology

I begin to suspect there are creatures
to match us, under the earth:

fish in the dew-ponds
dreaming us alive,

moles in a velvet landscape of thuds and sighs
decoding a muffled existence they would guess

was music, or a story being told
in cipher.
We are discontinuous

but knowable, after a fashion,
in such a world:

a shiver of noise at the spine, a fragment of scent,
a middle-ground of faith and hesitance,

touched by the same rain,
clenched in the same bright frost.

Signal Stop, near Horsley

Smoke in the woods
like someone walking in a silent film
beside the tracks.

A shape I recognize – not smoke, or not just smoke,
and not just snow on hazels
or fox-trails from the platform to the trees,

but winter, neither friend
nor stranger, like the girl I sometimes glimpse

at daybreak near the crossing, in a dress
of sleet and berries, gazing at the train.

Schadenfreude

How I suspected myself
of someone else,
when they caught me out by the kilns
with Sandra Gillespie,
reaching through zips and buttons for the damp
plumage of her undecided flesh,

and when I was far in the heat
of a May afternoon,
wading through duckweed and balsam to raid the nests
of moorhens and coots,
I knew in my secret heart
I was up to no good

and relished the inexplicable
malice of being,
holding the eggs in my mouth while I climbed the fence,
or crouched to our delicate barter, finding her out
through a vapour of perfume and salt
and the smoothing of cotton.

Pisces

She loved the wet whisper of silt
when tidewater seeped away
and the estuary rose to the town
through copper light,

a tender of glass and scales
and driftwood varnished with salt,
a circle she walked for miles
in search of shells,

picking starfish from a sheet
of silver tension, puzzled by the trails
of viscera, the threads of bloodless meat
and resurrected forms that had no names

but offered kinship, memory, regret,
a pulse between the water and her hand,
the feel of something old and buried deep,
heartbeat and vision quickening the sand.

Dialect

There were different words for dust:
one for the powdered film
of shading on a closed room's
windowsills,

and one for the inch-thick
layer of talcum and fibre
under the bed,

but nothing to describe the vividness
of rain-dark fur and flesh that shaped and gloved
the body of a fox beside the road,

and nothing for the presence still to come,
when wind and sunlight fretted at the bone,
cutting towards the basics of the form:
the knitted spine, the hunter's steady grin.

Aphasia in childhood

I

A room in a village schoolhouse: sprinklings of chalk and rice; wingbeats smoothing the windows under a fall of copper-leaf and prayer. Certain constants: quadratic equations; the word in Latin for table. Science in one book; history in the other.

The questions I asked all the time, but never aloud: where is the soul? what does it most resemble? I had an image of something transparent, a fine yet indestructible tissue of buttermilk or chitin. But nobody knew: there was only the sugar-and-clove-scented room, and the mail van passing through, dusted with pollen and ozone, bearing the witness of farmyards and distant towns, and they were *real*.

II

The evidence of home: hairs in the paintwork; broken fingernails between the carpet and the skirting-board. Traces; fibres; the smell of rubber gloves.

In the evening, with friends at the table, we spoke in anecdotes: the red stain of a haunting; a child in a nightdress; a picture of malice: sure-footed, graceful, walking around us on tiptoe. Mere entertainments, which no one would stop to believe.

Yet why repeat these histories if not for the peculiar sound of the victim? For the stoat in the soul: its pink-eyed wonder, its wistful desire for blood?

III

A shoebox of a life: gulls' eggs and bullets wrapped in the sweetness of Wills Whiffs; foxed snapshots of the classroom beauty, smiling at nothing, flirting across the years.

IV

It was always autumn. Each evening the village melted: steeples and slate roofs dissolving in sunset; willows and cedars plunging into dusk. I sat for hours in the radio's dusted warmth. I slept for months. By morning the gardens had reappeared; the fences smoked for miles in the gold suburbs; the hedges filled with water and jewelled birds.

I had lived so long. Maybe minutes. They sent me to school in a raincoat and colourless gloves.

V

Perfection arrives for the pleached hedges and the cress beds in frozen squares below the embankment. The parish map returns: steeples as landmarks; the old bounds of footpath and stream.

I am travelling a country of windows: a whiteness pressed to the glass as if the train was wrapped in iced velvet; the stations distilled to a glitter of frosted stone.

Memory clears: a series of lakes on maps, barely imagined, shrouded in oakwoods and moss.

VI

It keeps getting bigger. Everything points away from where I stand: new alleys scooped from light; street-names and waterglass hedges; paradigms for cherry tree and snow. That one day I spent in the woods, digging leaf-mould: I kept finding thin silvery threads of mildew that dissolved in the air, and I was sure, if I dug a few inches deeper, I would find a being which resembled me in every way, except that it would be white and etiolated, like a finger of bindweed growing under stone.

8 a.m. near Chilworth

Something has crossed the fields,
a series of claw prints
filling with plum-coloured water;

the stations run for miles:
a single whiteness threaded to the sun;
out in the woods

song-thrushes shiver the snow
from hazels, and the after-stain
of vixen is an echo from the book

of stories children tell on journeys home:
half-disbelieving, fingering the glass,
matching each flake of snow with inward brightness.

The pit town in winter

Everything would vanish in the snow,
fox bones and knuckles of coal
and dolls left out in the gardens,
red-mouthed and nude.

We shovelled and swept the paths,
but they melted away in the night
and the cars stood buried and dumb
on Fulford Road.

We might as well be lost, she said;
but I felt the neighbours dreaming in the dark,
and saw them wrapped in overcoats and scarves
on Sundays: careful, narrow-footed souls,
become the creatures of a sudden light,
amazed at how mysterious they were.

Like me, you sometimes waken
early in the dark
thinking you have driven miles
through inward country,

feeling around you still
the streaming trees and startled waterfowl
and summered cattle
swinging through your headlamps.

Sometimes you linger days
upon a word,
a single, uncontaminated drop
of sound; for days

it trembles, liquid to the mind,
then falls:
mere denotation,
dimming in the undertow of language.

Wrong

I

A swallowed nail. A trick with razor blades.

Round the allotments, four in the afternoon,
October: I was gouging out a face,
a jack-o'-lantern's grin of candlelight,
the jagged mouth, the nose, the death's-head eyes,
my knife too sharp, too reverently held

– that was my shed, my bunker, that smell of grease
and sacking, shrivelled tubers, rows of shrouded jars,
permethrin and flowers of sulphur,
phoxim and derris, rat poison's prussic blues,

a six by eight descent into the dark
where all I wanted was a raptor's grace,
an undertaker's skill with flesh and bone,
a single-mindedness, a sense of being.

II

Leaving the tattered parade
of bandsmen and footballers' wives,

and the clowns with their greasepaint smiles
and their buckets of silver,

I crossed the park
and found a borderline:

a wet sun, a muddy horizon,
cows standing out in a pasture

of thistles and dung.
For years I've wondered how it all went wrong,

how I went down,
how gulped air thickened to milk,

and how I was drained by that other
who found me there,

fluttering over my face
like a giant bat,

holding the knife that would cut through my flesh
like butter, then letting me fall

and turning away to the crowd
where he disappeared.

The rest like the far side of gas, that improbable
blue that dissolved, when I woke in the dentist's chair,

and a scatter of coins on the grass
in a cobweb of blood

red as the carnival mouths
of the drum majorettes

moving away
to the quiet erasure of distance.

III

I prayed for my father's death
on Sundays, when he mowed his patch of lawn,
his half-mad collie yapping at his heels,
his wife in the kitchen, snivelling over the onions.
I sat in our apple tree, hidden among the leaves,
my kneecaps and thumb-knuckles

crocheted with moss and bark
and willed him dead – the wish not mine alone,
but something of the house that drew me in:
that substance they found one winter, tucked in the flue,
all shinbone and whiskers, and nothing they could have named
with its winglike arms and a blue, almost questioning face,
a stitchwork of horsehair and mortar to hold it together,
mislaid all its life in a gap between snowfalls and cinders.

IV

There were small things I killed for pleasure:
ladybirds, craneflies, spiders and night-flying moths,
stubbing them out with my fingers
on icy glass,
or filling a jar with bees, to watch them
flicker and die.
I sprinkled lines of salt
on worms and slugs
and waited for the larger, sweeter kills:
the neighbour's Siamese, tied in a sack
and bubbling under the stream of Cotter's brook,
the poisoned owls, the dog lying dead in the road
– a logic that brings me here, to this neck of the woods
where no one will find him for days: a luckless child,
staring through water and leaves, and a remnant of warmth
bleeding away to the absence of love and mother.

V

I know this scene by heart:
the card from the victim arrives
from Margate or Clacton,
the voice-over comes through a blur
of milk-floats and Radio 1,
but the child is already dead
in a shallow grave,
a wet face covered with leaves,
the blue of his eyes
a promise for rats and magpies.
Then cut to an empty field
in a misty dawn,
the splash in the ditch, the headlamps,
the passing car –
I know he is only a prop
but I watch for a likeness,
that boy-child who's haunted the film
from the first bleak shot,
the photograph, the carnival parade
– and I think of his family
leaning to touch the screen
and find him again
or taste what they knew all along
was waiting to happen:
that sweetness that feathers the tongue;
that sense of themselves
as seen, like the people in movies.

Adam and Eve at Kinfauns

Angels with curls; death's-heads with open wings;
broken columns; ruins; hollow tombs.
Rabbits have disinterred the older dead,
burrowing down through rich, well-nourished earth
to ready shelter, sweetened with the dust
of locksmith and thief. Amongst the newer stones
a single grave is kept from common sight:
a young wife, by her husband's fond decree,
surrounded by yew, at the heart of a simple maze,
in topiary purdah.
The church itself is locked, its painted glass
surrendered to the dark, its bell
inert.
        I've come to see Adam and Eve,
carved in relief for a tenant whose name is lost
in ash-grey and rust-coloured lichens.
I never could believe the race was damned
for eating fruit,
our sin a want of knowledge and a native
disobedience.
Yet here it is, in all simplicity:
the apples smooth and large, the serpent gone,
Adam and Eve absurdly clothed
in kilts.
        I miss the snake.
The humans seem too innocent, alone,
like naughty children, acting on a dare.
The tree is rooted in a giant globe,
on which a shield or boss was once inscribed

with signs and words.
All that remains is *In Principio*,
hanging above the garden, in a cherub's
delicate span. Beyond the falling stone
the rabbit holes spill knucklebones and shins,
and empty sockets gaping in the rain.
There's no one buried here; though further on,
the hidden wife lies shrouded and unseen,
possessed, at last, by something more than love,
untouchable, beyond the pale of naming.

A distant cousin

I thought I could track you down
to one of those straw-covered huts
in Pittencrieff Park:
hairless and cicatriced, you would crouch in the rain,
gone native in the drip of rhododendrons.

Or, naked as bats in flight, we would meet in the ferns,
merging, then wheeling away
to the family outing:
my mother under her headscarf, smudged with mascara,
lining the others in rows for the Instamatic.

I thought I would find you submerged
in a hidden pool,
breathing through water, waiting to capture my soul,
the way our pictures only caught the forced
rehearsal of a smile, a milk-toothed grin,
the hint of a suspicion in our eyes
that someone was at home, while we were gone,
misting the windows, veiling the mirrors with stour.

Domestic

Late afternoon in October:
light feathers the kitchen walls,
finds long-lost cousins
in saucepans and colanders.
Footballers slide back and forth
on the muddy distance,
their voices splashing the neat
straight-furrow rattle of tractors
like slops. The new ram
is penned in the yard:
biblical in his hard
angle of heat and smell
and over-cautious, he stands
bowed, as if space itself
kept changing and had to be learned
in shifts and slants.
We sit indoors, alone,
pressed to the silence
like wasps to a window pane.
If we think of the homes we have known,
or stops between tunnels
when silence steps up to a train
through frost-printed trees,
if we think of old lovers or schools,
blank fields of ragwort and stones
or moss-scaled crab-apple lanes,
it barely shows.
At teatime, lamps go on
across the valley.

The marmalade cat stares in
from the window's gloaming
and, watched, we become what we seem
in the moth-coloured light,
like these figures we make in glass,
irredeemably bright.

Floating

I love this: how you weave our journey home
through narrow streets and hushed, expectant lanes,

as if you would have us lost, amidst the blur
of bricks and glass.

It's late July: the elms are shot with light;
the sycamores are glazed with honeydew.

We park above the town
and climb the hill:

the houses here are floating in the last
glimmer of day

and further up the street, beyond the church,
a woman is leaning out from an upper room

and singing along with the music that plays
behind her

– *If not for you* –

She's pleased with herself and sharing
more than the song with anyone who stops

to listen
and we wait to hear it out,
the man's voice under the woman's like a slowed

current, and the words a brief accord
between them: balanced; floating in the blue.

Burning a Woman

I WITCH WIFE

Sooner or later, you know she will make a spell
to feel the devil simmer in her flesh,

the moment of her pleasure incandescent:
foreign spirits burning in the dark

while others sleep. A woman in the house
is partly a hostage to fortune

and partly your mirror
shaken and brought to life

and no matter how often you try
to draw the thread of brightness from a son's

water and buttermilk skin,
his mother's language trickles off his tongue

and he stands in the yard like a girl
while you bring in the cattle,

snuffling and giggling,
calling each heifer by name.

II CARDIAC

My father is standing tall
in our narrow kitchen:

blood on the table,
a litter of eggs and glass

on the clouded floor.
He's clutching a fistful of coins

like a drowning swimmer,
drunk again, and dead these seven years,

but still, in my frightened dreams,
immersed in anger;

looking for someone to blame
that he might be pardoned

and go down under the flood
with his heart intact.

III A PINT OF MILD

I liked how he said it, as if it were
honey, or dew,
or something you drank with the ladies:
a secret pleasure.
It made me believe he had come
from another language,
with names for the colour of pines
in the morning sun
or how a woman smells when giving birth,
and no historic past
or future tense,
only a present of streetlamps and empty roads,
and men spilling out of the light, in the evening air,
or wandering into the blue
of a different story.

IV LIKE FATHER

Let me imagine you capable of love
and transformation,

the dream of a man made subtle, or straight as a die,
a judge of character, a connoisseur,

whatever you thought you had lost, when you made me
listen for years to stories I couldn't believe.

I know how you shift and start when I'm passing the time,
walking from church to church in a foreign city,

making coffee, talking on the phone,
clumsy, helpless, sorry for myself,

and just the man you wanted me to be,
good for nothing, skilled in self-deceit,

punished so often for errors I never made
I'm blind to my worst mistakes, and beyond redemption.

V BURNING A WOMAN

A dark afternoon. The houses on Eastwood Road
are Belgian, all of a sudden,
where someone has lit a fire in a corner of privet;

damp and slow, a fleece of yellow smoke
clings to the leaves like mildew; I think of the time
my father stood in the yard at Handcross Court

burning my mother, a fortnight after she died:
her only coat, her witch's broom of scarves,
bonnets and nylons, ribbons of freshwater pearls.

I’ve worked from this faded blueprint and got it wrong
time after time,
thinking I see him wandering back and forth,

trailing dresses, stoking the fire with shoes
to watch them burn,
then seeing myself, next morning in the rain,

probing the ashes for salvage, for hairpins and beads,
a litter of buttons, like eggs going cold in the nest,
or the précis of stitchwork and feathers she once made good.

The old gods

Now they are condemned
to live in cracks,
in bubbles of plaster and rust,
and spiders' webs
behind the furniture:

speaking a derelict language
to empty space,
sealed with the vapour
in bottles, closed in the blown
robins' eggs
in some abandoned loft.

Each has its given power.
Each has its hearth, its secret,
its local name,
and each has its way of learning
the skill of return,
the science of bleeding through, when anger or fear
is fuzzing the surface,
making us dizzy and whole.

The solitary in autumn

I am standing out in the yard
at the end of October,
building a fire of drifted leaves and twigs,
letters for kindling, apples amongst the flames,
the last of summer, dropping through the embers.

There is that perfume in the shade
that is almost viburnum,
traces of snow and water in the light,
a blankness along the canal
that waits to be filled

and, given the silence, given the promise of frost,
I might have welcomed this as something else:
the taste of windfalls moving on the stream
a faint god's partial emergence
through willow and alder.

The riverbank darkens and fades.
The garden recovers its creatures: slow worms and frogs
and blackbirds sifting the dead
in the still of the damsons.
Across the river, evening bleeds the trees,

my neighbour's garden blurs to smoke and rain;
sometimes I think that someone else is there,
standing in his own yard, raking leaves,
or bending to a clutch of twigs and straw
to breathe a little life into the fire.

The myth of the twin

Say it moved when you moved:
a softness that rose in the ground
when you walked, or a give in your step,
the substance that Virgil saw
in the shadows under our feet;

and say it was out there, out in the snow,
meshed with the birdsong and light
the way things are real: a blackbird, a scribble of thorns,
a quickening into the moment, the present tense,

and the way that a stumbling or sudden
rooting in authenticity is not
the revelation of a foreign place,
but emptiness, a stillness in the frost,
the silence that stands in the birchwoods, the common soul.

Robert Crawford

Opera

Throw all your stagey chandeliers in wheelbarrows and move
them north
To celebrate my mother's sewing-machine
And her beneath an eighty-watt bulb, pedalling
Iambs on an antique metal footplate
Powering the needle through its regular lines,
Doing her work. To me as a young boy
That was her typewriter. I'd watch
Her hands and feet in unison, or read
Between her calves the wrought-iron letters:
SINGER. Mass-produced polished wood and metal,
It was a powerful instrument. I stared
Hard at its brilliant needle's eye that purred
And shone at night; and then each morning after
I went to work at school, wearing her songs.

Photonics

We're a new technology, a system that weds
Lasers; no electronics; no gob-drops
Of glass fibre to be teased and spun; just conjugate-phasing
Turning constant signals into rings of light,
A burgh packed with brilliant marriages

Strong the way a towerblock in an earthquake zone
Rocks and quivers, floating erect
On its bed of underground gravels; we're making discoveries,
Simplifying, unbuckling at the waist,
Unbuttoning the two pearl buttons at your throat,

Till we lie where the Giant flung his shining Causeway
Over gaunt blue water into these small, sweet hills;
We meet as clearly as two beams in a saltire
Bonded at the centre, having each
Come through all the R & D to run on light.

The Dalswinton Enlightenment

Patrick Miller's first iron vessel, the world's
First steamship is swanning across Dalswinton Loch.
A landscape painter, Alexander Nasmyth
Perches on deck beside his good friend, Robert Burns.

It's a calm, clear morning. The painter will later invent
The compression rivet, and work out the axial arrangement
Between propeller and engine. The poet will write about the
  light
Of science dawning over Europe, remembering how

Cold sun struck Pat's boat that October day at Dalswinton
When the churning paddles articulated the loch
In triumphant metre, and the locals made some cracks
Almost as if they were watching a ship of fools.

Scotland in the 1890s

'I came across these facts which, mixed with others . . .'
Thinking of Helensburgh, J. G. Frazer
Revises flayings and human sacrifice;
Abo of the Celtic Twilight, St Andrew Lang
Posts him a ten-page note on totemism
And a coloured fairy book – an Oxford man
From Selkirk, he translates Homer in his sleep.

'When you've lived here, even for a short time,
Samoa's a bit like Scotland – there's the sea . . .
Back in Auld Reekie with a pen that sputtered
I wrote my ballad, "Ticonderoga" or
"A Legend of the West Highlands", then returned
To King Kalakaua's beach and torches –
You know my grandfather lit Lismore's south end?'

Mr Carnegie has bought Skibo Castle.
His union jack's sewn to the stars and stripes.
James Murray combs the dialect from his beard
And files slips for his massive *Dictionary*.
Closing a fine biography of mother,
Remembering Dumfries, and liking boys,
James Barrie, caught in pregnant London silence,
Begins to conceive the Never Never Land.

John Logie Baird

When it rained past Dumbarton Rock
You skipped Classics for a motorbike exploration

Of the Clyde's slow Raj. In sodden memsahibs' gardens
Hydrangeas unfurled into fibre-optics.

A dominie lochgellied you once
For pronouncing 'Eelensburgh' like those wild, untouchable
  tinks

Who, if they could see your biker's career from today's
Long distance, would snigger. A socialist most famous for

Inventing an undersock, screened from douce cousins,
Under bamboos at a small jam factory

Near Port of Spain you achieved television
And paid for it. At the trials a boy called Reith

Risen from your old class shook hands, then wrote you off.
You worked. When World War II ended

Baird equipment broadcast victory in the Savoy
But not one diner said cheerio when you faded,

An obsolete wallah, edited out, still beaming
One hand outstretched across those Clydelike waves.

Syrophenician

You were the Syrophenician woman
Arguing with God, a dog among the Jews.
Glare islanded and baked you, shadows turned

On your crazy daughter. Border squatter
Between yes and no, you persisted, stubborn bitch,
Till your answer ripened, like the nod to Zacchaeus in his tree

Or Loch Lomond light stunning a houseboat's windows
Into juddery polythene, a whiteout moment
When the one whom you loved most was healed.

Inner Glasgow

You were a small red coat among the pit bings
That aren't there now, between Cambuslang
And Shettleston, with *Tell Me Why, Look and Learn*;

The quays have altered, liners replaced by jasmine;
Where docks are cultivated, hard nostalgia
Steam-rivets us to ghosts we love, in murals

Where everybody looks the same and sings
Of oppression, smokes, drinks lager, shouts out 'fuck'.
Shops sell us. Entrepreneurs' industrial

Museums postcard grime; we're pseudo-Griersonned.
But you refuse these foisted images, stay
Too true, still here, grown up in your red coat.

My inner Glasgow, you don't leave me, I
Do not leave you. A tubular steel frontage, roadcones
Flash towards us like the tiny folded pictures

In pop-up books, the lovely, lovely details
Too close to label art, that bring on laughter
When words cut out their starter motor, leaving us

Idling beside a cloudless firth. Those shorelights
Spread beyond Millport, beckon us to marry,
To lie along the bowsprits of our lives.

The Approach

Floating, floating. In the tall dairy
Of the floods beyond, ruled with a grid of days,
Pigeons call. You remain like honey
Approaching through the hinterland, with deer abrupt
In front of the headlamps. You can absorb
Long novels of sleep and thermocouples
As the waves crash in. Night lowers its landing gear
And turns on one side. Over the telephone
Yesterday may be recounted.
Evening brindles, waiting outside the church,
Pine smells blend with the scent of cooked food.
What time is it? Like oystercatchers, breath
On the flutehole quickens us, makes us persist;
It is approaching in boatsongs, it is approaching
With loyalty running in new shoes
Through a soaking meadow, pollen-drift
Sloughed off on your bare knees.
Each of us has the laser on the disc's rotation
Dispensing arias, zither's, moon-shaped lute's.
Feathered with a tang of salt, it approaches
Floating, about to be:
Ours, when the time is proper, silent
At the sea's edge, and the surf breeze brings you
Laughing ashore from the Gulf Stream at Machrihanish.

Scotland

Semiconductor country, land crammed with intimate
expanses,
Your cities are superlattices, heterojunctive
Graphed from the air, your cropmarked farmlands
Are epitaxies of tweed.

All night motorways carry your signal, swept
To East Kilbride or Dunfermline. A brightness off low
headlands
Beams-in the dawn to Fife's interstices,
Optoelectronics of hay.

Micro-nation. So small you cannot be forgotten,
Bible inscribed on a ricegrain, hi-tech's key
Locked into the earth, your televised Glasgows
Are broadcast in Rio. Among circuitboard crowsteps

To be miniaturized is not small-minded.
To love you needs more details than the Book of Kells –
Your harbours, your photography, your democratic intellect
Still boundless, chip of a nation.

A Scottish Assembly

Circuitry's electronic tartan, the sea,
Libraries, fields – I want the lot

To fly off and scatter, but most of all
Always to come home to roost

In this unkempt country where a handicapped printer,
Engraver of dog collars, began with his friends

The ultimate encyclopedia.
Don't expect any rhyme or reason

For Scotland remaining an explosion reversed
Or ordinariness a fruited vine

Or why I came back here to choose my union
On the side of the ayes, remaining a part

Of this diverse assembly – Benbecula, Glasgow, Bow of Fife –
Voting with my feet, and this hand.

Rain

A motorbike breaks down near Sanna in torrential rain,
Pouring loud enough to perforate limousines, long enough
To wash us to Belize. Partick's
Fish-scaled with wetness. Drips shower from foliage, cobbles,
tourists
From New York and Düsseldorf at the tideline
Shoes lost in bogs, soaked in potholes, clarted with glaur.
An old woman is splashed by a bus. A gash
In cloud. Indians
Arrived this week to join their families and who do not feel
Scottish one inch push onwards into a drizzle
That gets heavy and vertical. Golf umbrellas
Come up like orchids on fast-forward film; exotic
Cagoules fluoresce nowhere, speckling a hillside, and
plump

Off dykes and gutters, overflowing
Ditches, a granary of water drenches the shoulders
Of Goatfell and Schiehallion. Maps under perspex go bleary,
Spectacles clog, Strathclyde, Tayside, Dundee
Catch it, fingers spilling with water, oil-stained
As it comes down in sheets, blows
Where there are no trees, snow-wet, without thought of the
morrow.
Weddings, prunes, abattoirs, strippers, Glen Nevis, snails
Blur in its democracy, down your back, on your breasts.
In Kilmarnock a child walks naked. A woman laughs.
In cars, in Tiree bedrooms, in caravans and tenements,
Couples sleeved in love, the gibbous Govan rain.

Alba Einstein

When proof of Einstein's Glaswegian birth
First hit the media everything else was dropped:
Logie Baird, Dundee painters, David Hume – all
Got the big E. Physics documentaries
Became peak-viewing; Scots publishers hurled awa
MacDiarmid like an overbaked potato, and swooped
On the memorabilia: *Einstein Used My Fruitshop*,
Einstein in Old Postcards, Einstein's Bearsden Relatives.
Hot on their heels came the A. E. Fun Park,
Quantum Court, Glen Einstein Highland Malt.
Glasgow was booming. Scotland rose to its feet
At Albert Suppers where The Toast to the General Theory
Was given by footballers, panto-dames, or restaurateurs.
In the US an ageing lab-technician recorded
How the Great Man when excited showed a telltale glottal
stop.
He'd loved fiddlers' rallies. His favourite sport was curling.
Thanks to this, Scottish business expanded
Endlessly. His head grew toby-jug-shaped,
Ideal for keyrings. He'd always worn brogues.
Ate bannocks in exile. As a wee boy he'd read *The Beano.*
His name brought new energy: our culture was solidly based
On pride in our hero, The Universal Scot.

THE FLYTING OF CRAWFORD AND HERBERT

STERT HEAR

Daft Herbert, wi yir pigtail Scoats
A' vitriol agin Dundee,
Yir poetry's a crood o quotes
Ye jist tak in fur B & B

An fling oot tae the *n*th degree.
Puir Japs in Oban, lost an cauld,
Picasso, Luzi, Valéry
'll nae gang hame when they are tauld

But bizz roon readers lik big clegs
Pisenin the pure auld Scoatish bluid
That poo'ered Culloden's airms an legs –
Ye're varicose, maun! Whit's the guid

O sayin yir *Gairfush* jouks an dives,
Yir 'Parallax' gangs oan an oan . . .?
Ther's nae a line o yon survives
A blin maun's gaze. Yir lang 'ochone'

Soons jist lik wattered English. Ach,
Yir wurds, yir herr, yir claithes are nocht but chaff.
Wee nipcaik, scatterloonsiebodach,
Repent noo! Shut yir gob! Piss aff!

'Parallax' – an obscure laxative emission by Herbert, running to an uncountable number of lines; nipcaik – a mean person; scatterloonsiebodach – confused young person of little wit (coinage).

HERBERT'S REPONE

Caa me a precious pickthank wad yi,
younkir in Scots o hoo mony months?
an think Eh'll bide easy an no scad yi
whilst you gae sea-queasy owre
whit? an immane wheen
o bardic clunkertonies
that'll lend a pizend tentacil or fowre
til aa thi faan phonies
an fossils, thi rumorous drunkelews
that flaithir up thi scene
wi spittle-tattle; lourdanes an lossils
yi'd hae me scrieve *fur* an no *at*?

Luke til yir ain hauf-shat tamschooleries!
whit toss-potly vility is here
o 'science'? Crympilt, rympilt dooleries,
rugatous sheets squeezed oot in fear
o bein left ahint by physicists
wi naethin mair ti sey
til 'genius' crottils uts een lyk cysts
or suns, an shaws them all thi wey
oot o thi Uncertainty Principal
intil a newel dey –
an you, darklin's darra, think this better
than *la pureté du Non-être*!

Eh amna precious thi wey you're ootir-specious,
but fule-large and eagerd-o-tung;
Eh wadna whistir til a philistine's vant
or waant tae be Scoatlan's musicant
gin thon wiz imaginaishun's bung:
Eh amna wun tae lick fat fae aa gash-beards –

Sae quit yir mafflin fur scatterlins
or quap aff this quaquaversal chalice;
meh saporate malice'll swap aff
yir todlichin feet, an yir tung-betroosht heid
fae abune yi –
yi hauf-fisst groat, yi thin-cheekit chitty-fiss;
dje waant ma 'wattered' wurds tae droon yi?

Repone – reply; pickthank – thief; younkir – youth; scad – scald; immane – dangerous; wheen – small number; clunkertonies – jellyfish; rumorous drunkelews – those obsessed with position and gossip; flaithir – obscure with wheedling; lourdanes an lossils – worthless oafs; vility – vileness; dooleries – very sad things; rugatous – crumpled, rumpled; crottils – clots; newel – novel; darklin's darra – the hooks and sinkers attached to a hand-line let down in the dark; whister – whistle drily; vant – boast; musicant – composer of small competence; gash-beards – snobs; mafflin – muttering in agreement; scatterlins – creatures of no consequence; quap aff – knock back; quaquaversal – dipping outwards in all directions from a centre; saporate – flavoursome; swap aff – chop off; todlichen – learning to toddle; tung-betroosht – too ready with the tongue.

A TIP ABOOT HERBERT

ACH, Sherbet-Herbert, sugarallie-mou'd,
Yir lang tung blak fae Wattie Cairns's brogues,
Yi'll nae lick me wi aw yon tun o stewed
Auld prunes – yir 'sangs'! Yir neolith pirogue's

Whambled wi wattir. *Yi* tak saalt an droon,
Pukin up firths o filth, but nae oan *me*
Whan Ah cum doon the wattir fur tae croon
Yir Mortal Memry: 'He wiz aye at sea

In aw he wrote – sae R.I.P.' – or's near
Tae P. as aebody expecks wha kens
Yon foul stramash yir vast mou generates;
That muckil bus-park o a mou, wi hens
Peckin roon molars, an spittil-wattir-rates

Jist astronomick! Mou an mou an mou!
Ther's nae a LITRY GUIDE fur years tae cum
Wull miss yon Fingal's Cave-*manqué* – yir mou
('A true Blak Hale.' 'A daurk titanic lum . . .') –

Makin thi puir Scoats launscape aw aroon
Ae dumpin-groon fur thi warld's B.O. 'drous skip
Tae disgoarge tripe an swell yon garbage foon'
I'yir pit-mirk mou Ah christen HERBERT'S TIP!

Sugarallie – liquorice; mou – mouth; Wattie Cairns – Walter Cairns, Literature Director, Scottish Arts Council, who has kept the national purse totally intact in the face of Herbert's ceaseless assaults; stramash – uproar, tumult; lum – chimney; pit-mirk – pitch-dark.

COUP DE POING

Ah, therr's yir West-coast cant,
yi Frasir-in-Graham's pants,
yi Muir-in-MacDiarmid's socks:
therr's yir nidus o Glescae cock!

Yi waant yir ain Criterionic case
o draw-latch stealth fae raw-datchied makars
aa guizerd in thon nebulon o noth,
Thi Concise Warld o Crawford;
reality rabbd o health an scouth –
an since yi cannae afford
tae plaistir thi haill place wi yir haimald fiss,
yi've sent aa rufflirs aff ti thi knackirs.
But whit's Limbo fur you Glescae bimbos is
a leal-leid-lubbirs' (seal an cypher-sirens') Libertad
o googy wurds in freedom;
a mair-nor-moisty Easterly you caa bad
becoz yi ken ut's yir feedom –

Weel then, is ut ill tae pend in
thi pseudo-miasmic skin
o this buik, wi a vilipendin
Miamese twin?

Aye, but Eh'll no bide easy!

Ur yi feart o thi glaw yi fulzie-can
ti ma sprouthy flauchtir-spad?
Yi freachy-froochy garglyum, yi tad;
yi gypical lilti-cock, yi breeze o scran,
yi merest smellfeast o 'verse';
yir gneck-i-thi-neck's ony galschich
that disna groofil in yir hashlich
o cautionriness cleidit as 'terse' –
but thon's yir gallows'-loop:
meh waatir-cords ur roond yi, yi glupe
that's haarld-i-thi-thrappil, yi javel o consternaishun;

yi ken Eh'm true, an thon's yir terrificaishun!

Coup de poing – the finishing stroke in Scottish ping pong, usually delivered with a neolithic hand-axe; nidus – nest; draw-latch – thiefly; stealth – plunder; raw-datchied – possessed of brutal secret insights; nebulon o noth – a whirl of gases, signifying nothing; scouth – abundance, scope; haimald – domesticated; googy – fecund; feedom – presage of death; vilipendin – insulting; glaur – primal ooze; fulzie-can – a vessel for holding night-soil; sprouthy – sprouting; flauchtir-spad – spade for cutting peats; freachy-froochy – spoiled in the making, faded, brittle and rotten; garglyum – fledgeling; tad – tadpole; gypical – characteristically foolish; lilti-cock – a jerky walker; scran – miscellaneous scraps of food; smellfeast – a meal comprised solely of the smell of food; gneck-i-thi-neck – source of irritation; galschich – sweetmeat, anything exotic; hashlich – refuse; cleidit – clothed; glupe – vast, empty cave; haarld-i-thi-thrappil – hoarsely throated; javel – fool.

Ah Waant . . .

Ah waant yon guid aucht that's weet as olours, rerr
As spluntin acors thi Mojave – mair thumblickin,
Prollin thumbs hurry burry aw owre yi, wi nae
Hurkle-durkle; stramash o reists an shanks,

Loup ourweillin inventars o loo:
Loofs, lonyngs, skirdoch o orising, red.
An mornin a poddasway ayont thi hairst-rig,
A souple, souple dawn.

I want that good intimate possession that's wet as herbs liked by swans, rare as running after girls at night across the Mojave – more making of bargains by licking thumbs, licking and striking thumbs in confused hurry all over you, with no sluggishness in bed; disturbance of restive waiting insteps and legs, leap exceeding inventories of love: palms of the hand, narrow passageways, flirting of arising, spawning place. And morning a garment whose warp and woof are silk, beyond the couple who reap together at harvest, a supple, cunning dawn.

Day Cowps . . .

Day cowps, swaagin,
Simmer-flaws pasperin thi milkmaid's path
Whan thi pap o thi hass, eefauld as a rock-doo,
Shaks sangs ayont thi earny-couligs.

In yon king's weathir Ah tak yir haun
By thi pirliewinkie an get yi up tae thi taing.
Oor boadies mell lik thi raise-net fishin,
Lik a kindlie tae Adam's wine.

Day spills over, fluttering like a bird's wing, ground mists that rise from the soil on a hot day turning the Milky Way to samphires, when the uvula, honest as a wild pigeon, shakes songs beyond the tumuli. In these exhalations rising from the earth on a warm day I take your hand by the smallest finger and go with you up to the headland. Our bodies grow intimate like that kind of fishing where part of the net rises and flows and subsides with the tide, like an ancestral claim to water.

Simultaneous Translation

It fills up the pause when you finish speaking,
Or even before you've stopped,

Gets between the chewy biro and the word-processor,
Between 'Yours sincerely' and your name.

Other times you walk right into it
At Aberfeldy, going over the Highland Line

Towards something you can't understand,
Also somewhere you've been.

Gaels in Glasgow, Bangladeshis in Bradford,
Negotiators, opera-buffs, tourists:

This is where we all live now,
Wearing something like a Sony Walkman,

Hearing another voice every time we speak.
A girl opens her mouth and an Oxbridge bass

Is talking in English. What is she really saying?
Already her finger is starting to creep

Closer to the binding of a parallel text,
Between the lines, then crossing over.

Mary of Bernera

Mary of Bernera, doe-eyed Mary, Mary of the songs, you are as honey and your breasts are as sweet white apples, but I no longer find you erotically attractive. When the Minister of the Free Church preached his sermon against my hands inside your bathing dress I was in the kirk and was traumatized by it. All the energies which our love consumed I now devote to marketing edible seaweeds. Mary of Bernera, doe-eyed Mary, Mary of the songs, though I cannot be with you I have your eyelashes in a small box. I carry it with me to the sea's edge and on the shingle. I who was your lover now sell seaweed to old crofters from a Renault van. There is a matchbox in my overalls. Think on me, Mary of the songs.

Prayer

Upstream from shattered urban lintels
Lost crofts are soft as new bread.

That dripping tap in the one-walled kitchen
Reminds someone there will be a need
Of water before and after.

Sin to imagine a perfect world
Without embarrassment, rain, or prayer.
A hand is clasping my other hand

In a dark place that has to be got through
On a wing and. Listen to this.

Talkies

Already there is gossip in Hollywood
About something new. Even the stars will need tests.

In the beginning was the caption,
Ringlets, a balletic flow of knees;

Crowds opened their mouths, then closed them.
Now some will never be heard of again

If between camera-loving, soundless lips
Is a foreign accent, or that timbre of voice which means

The microphone doesn't like you.
Friends swell into enormous heart-throbs:

Their voices are good. 'Retraining?
Let me get you another drink.'

At the neat wrought-iron table,
Legs crossed, she stares at the studio,

A hangar, a camp, a silo. Work
Means something else now, something other

Than what she set her heart on, black and white silk, panache.
With a longer lifespan she might become

A nostalgia executive, a Last of the, a rediscovery.
But the dates are wrong; leaving her speechless

At this technology crackling over California
Eagerly, far out of sight.

The First Judgement

The eyes will be judged first
Before they can return to their bodies.

There's an enormous queue of them, a voice asking
Did you see on television

Poor people with captions in front
Explaining what they said in their dialects?

What did you video? When you went outside
Did you avert yourselves from anything odd?

The eyes look at each other. This

Isn't what they expected. They want to argue,
But they are no longer linked up to mouths.

They want to elect a brilliant spokesperson,
Without hands. They want

To be able to make various deferred gestures,
To wink, to authorize immediate payment,

To shut themselves tightly against the light.
But they have no bodies, no eyelids.

Eyes who watched television, and eyes who were watched
Stare at each other. Some of them burst into tears.

Others know that without tearducts
They are no longer able to cry.

Eyes who are crying, and dry, clear eyes
Examine one another intently.

Right, says the voice, you've been judged.

Bond

In his late eighties he still took his dog to the cinema. They went to see *You Only Live Twice*. His daughter-in-law would get very embarrassed; 'Someone's got to sit on that seat afterwards.' Ears cocked, the collie perched on the velour. A man in the row behind leant forward, gave a tap on the shoulder. 'Hey, mister, is yur dug enjoyin the pictchur?' 'Aye, son, can ye no tell? He's seen all the James Bonds. He feels it's a shame it's no still Sean Connery but.'

The Humanity Classroom

Sitting there, I was a comma in the bible;
On either side great generations of talk.

The word means Latin. Stubbornly at the Uni
They went on calling it Humanity.

Before my time, in mid-*Aeneid*
A woman at the lectern under big oil portraits

Threw open a window, leaned out listening
To riveters at work in the shipyards.

Anne of Green Gables

Short, moneyless summers at West Kilbride you sat out
On the back steps with a view of the outside toilet
Reading the Anne books, one after the datestamped next,

Anne of Windy Willows, Anne of Avonlea,
Anne of the Island, Anne's House of Dreams.
No books were ever as good as these

From West Kilbride Public Library
That always had to go back.
When we got married, one by one

You bought the whole set, reading them through. At first
I was jealous when you sat not speaking,
Then put the books away on your own shelf.

'"How white the moonlight is tonight," said Anne
Blythe to herself.' At first
I was jealous. Not now.

A Quiet Man

My best friend at school, then at university
Turned out to be gay

Which was fine, but left me somehow
Lonely. I knew I'd never

Be a ladies' man, or a man's man either.
Unpubby, hating cigarette smoke,

I took out girls to the Art Galleries,
Typing them sonnets. I mooned,

Living in fear some reintroduced
National Service sergeant major

Would noisily break me in two.
Odd those sergeant majors now

Are gender fossils, and here I am
Washing the dishes but not doing ironing,

Married. Evolved from my all-male school
And that bristling, women-only college

I lived in later for years,
I stand off-balance, mumbling something

About our wee son's future, his stripy flag
A dishtowel my Dad brandished when he made me

Like him an in-between, quiet man,
Homo silens, a missing link.

Chaps

With his Bible, his Burns, his brose and his baps
Colonel John Buchan is one of the chaps,
With his mother, his mowser, his mauser, his maps,
Winston S. Churchill is one of the chaps.

Chaps chaps chaps chaps
Chaps chaps chaps chaps

Rebecca Mphalele is one of the chaps,
Ezekiel Ng is one of the chaps,
Queenie Macfadzean is one of the chaps,
Kayode Nimgaonkar is one of the chaps.

Chaps chaps chaps chaps
Chaps chaps chaps chaps

Oxfordy chaps, Cambridgey chaps,
Glasgowy chaps, Harrovian chaps,
Oxfordy chaps, Cambridgey chaps,
Oxfordy chaps, Cambridgey chaps.

Chaps chaps chaps chaps
Chaps chaps chaps chaps

The sergeant's a chap, the rifle's a chap,
The veldt is a chap, the heather's a chap,
A great JCR of them tossing their caps
Like schoolboys at Eton dyed red on the maps.

Chaps chaps chaps chaps
Chaps chaps chaps chaps

The porthole's a chap, the cannon's a chap,
The Haigs and the Slessors, the Parks are all chaps,
Mungos and Maries, filling the gaps
In the Empire's red line that can never collapse.

Chaps chaps chaps chaps
Chaps chaps chaps chaps

Lord Kitchener needs them to pose for his snaps
Of Ypres and Verdun with chaps' heads in their laps
Singing Gilbert and Sullivan or outlining traps
To catch rowdies at Eights Week, next year perhaps.

Chaps chaps chaps chaps
Chaps chaps chaps chaps

The war memorial's a chap, the codebook's a chap,
The wind is a chap, the horse is a chap
The knitters, the padres, the limbs are all chaps
From Hawick and Africa, poppies are chaps

Chaps chaps chaps chaps
Chaps chaps chaps chaps

Name and Address Supplied

My Edwardian friend Arthur Farquharson
Lived in college three enormous years
With his ties, shirts, trousers, jackets,
Underwear and socks all neatly sporting
An embroidered label, ARTHUR FARQUHARSON,
Then the college address and postcode.
Six months into his college residence
His case was stolen. The hopeful thief,
Finding no lap-tops, cash, or videos,
Just unironed shirts and old school ties,
Beery sportsjackets, Henry Tudor longjohns,
And Scott of the Antarctic vests,
Hurled the slashed suitcase in a shot-putter's arc
Over the windswept, flooded field
Just off the ringroad, so Arthur's most intimate whites
Fell among nettles, a cross between rumpled snowflakes
And parachutists dropped at Arnhem.
For months afterwards tall, po-faced
Students would amble into the college
With a plastic bag of Arthur's smalls
All birdshit and sodden cotton,
Harvested from scrubland or gutters or animals' burrows,
Then when Arthur slunk back from work each evening
Weary and keeping close to the wall,
The alert porter stood in reception
Brandishing a pair of weathered, just recognizable
Fridtjof Nansen Patent Hyperthermals,
Thundering into the mellow evening
With its arm-in-arm couples, its cricket elevens,

'Mr Farquharson, surely these must be yours?'
 I mention this because once my mother
In a bout of implacable maternal pride
Labelled every piece of my clothing
ROBERT CRAWFORD, HOLYWELL MANOR
And though I haven't lived for years
In that graduate centre, I still get up
On anxious mornings, peering inside
Old socks and cardigans in bleached midwinter
To see what exactly they say.

Male Infertility

Slouched there in the Aston Martin
On its abattoir of upholstery

He escapes
To the storming of the undersea missile silo,

The satellite rescue, the hydrofoil
That hits the beach, becoming a car

With Q's amazing state-of-the-art,
State-of-the-art, state-of-the-art . . .

Suddenly he has this vision
Of a sperm in a boyhood sex-ed film

As a speargun-carrying, tadpole-flippered frogman
Whose visor fills up with tears,

And of living forever in a dinnerjacket
Fussier and fussier about what to drink,

Always, 'Shaken, not stirred.'
Chlorine-blue bikinis, roulette tables, waterskiing –

Show me that scene in *Thunderball*
Where James Bond changes a nappy.

Ripening

My mother buys my dad a new tweed jacket
Very rarely, always at the sales.

Upstairs in one of two mahogany wardrobes
He hangs it like a shot bird to be cured,

New for a decade, it takes on the smell
Of jackets round it, his scent, the reek of mothballs.

On coathangers, suspended in the dark,
Herringbone accepts the gift of waiting.

Unseasoned pockets sense how ripened pockets
Unfold receipts and stones, then yield up string.

As they get worn, my mother schools thinned elbows
In leather patches, and younger jackets learn

To renounce fashion long before he wears them.
'Is that a new jacket?' 'Yes,' he says, 'it is.'

Us

Silence parked there like a limousine;
We had no garage and we had no car.

Dad polished shoes, boiled kettles for hot-water bottles,
And mother made pancakes, casseroles, lentil soup

On her New World cooker, its blue and cream
Obsolete before I was born.

I was a late, only child, campaigning
For 33 r.p.m. records.

Dad brought food parcels from City Bakeries
In crisp brown paper, tightly bound with string.

So many times he felt annoyed
When a visitor left without shutting the gate.

Now someone will bid for, then clear these rooms,
Stripping them of us. We were that floral wallpaper,

That stuck serving-hatch, radiograms polished and broken,
Dogeared carpet-tiles that understood us,

Our locked bureau, crammed with ourselves.

Spirit Country

Over a long Bank Holiday weekend
Letters mature in dark insides of pillarboxes.
On the familiar stroll home from the box
Senders insert an extra sentence,
Alter a promise or the name of an addressee.
Cambuslang, Cambuslang

Where bedroom scenes are protected by sandstone
Villas set well back from the road
Among firs with cones the size of pint glasses,
Sycamores, monkey-puzzles,
Lilacs, broom bushes, self-sufficient redcurrants,
Cambuslang, Cambuslang

Where everyone except blood relations
In Canada, South Africa, or Greenock
Was so local on that dark afternoon
When I knelt down to crayon my first Christmas cards
They needed no stamps above the addresses,
Cambuslang, Cambuslang.

As I walked through the snow to deliver them,
Climbing the steep path at 22 Brownside Road,
I crossed a front garden lit by cold yellow rectangles,
Light-shadows thrown from the livingroom windows
Where the McNeills sat chatting, curtains not yet drawn,
Cambuslang, Cambuslang.

A teenager, I had to imagine
Our left-bank-of-the-Clyde photographers' studios,
Bortsch-specked carpets in the foyer of our Polish Theatre,

Our Art Gallery, our sandstone Opera House,
Our reopened cinema, our Tourist Office, our tourists,
Cambuslang, Cambuslang.

Instead, we had a children's library,
Eight nearby churches, an annual Flower Show
In Cambuslang Institute with miniature gardens
Laid out on tea-trays, their six-inch garden paths
Gravelled with lentils, shrubbery sprigs of parsley,
Cambuslang, Cambuslang

In bonsai form, mum's handbag mirror
Forming still water on an ornamental pond,
Pallisade fencing of old ice-lolly sticks,
A fantasy summerhouse tiled with melon seeds.
I won cups for those gardens on trays,
Cambuslang, Cambuslang

Whose high tea ceremonies governed a suburban cuisine
Of digestive biscuits, Cream Crackers, Jaffa Cakes
Expensive as doilies, in a serviette culture
Rich in shortbread and clean tablecloths'
Ancestral napkins married to napkin rings,
Cambuslang, Cambuslang

Whose leaves were pre-decimal, every bike a Raleigh
Insulated with privet. I visited
By prior appointment short ladies in Central Avenue
Whose dark-varnished lounges denied the post-War world.
Frail and marginal, they pronounced proudly 'Kembusleng'.
Cambuslang, Cambuslang,

Ha-ha Harry Lauder had lived once in Hamilton Drive
Where but-and-ben bungalows looked built to house
His bakelite songs still lying fragile

In a big, black doctor's bag of records
On our front-room lino near Fingal's Cave,
Cambuslang, Cambuslang,

From Mendelssohn's Hebrides, Handel's Largo,
The Arrival of the Queen of Sheba;
When she came I would watch her progress
Through long-sashed front windows, her trousers brighter
Than any of our curtains. She'd soon be here,
Cambuslang, Cambuslang,

From East Kilbride to carry me away
From my pals with their tricycles and Scalextric sets,
Genesis and Status Quo,
Who suddenly now are living in Cairo
And whose fathers have collapsed like a trellis.
Cambuslang, Cambuslang,

She is coming to carry me off from the bogey
I was always about to plummet on down Douglas Drive.
Somehow none of my friends can compete
With her intellect or vagina.
I'm walking to marry her, in a dark blue suit,
Cambuslang, Cambuslang,

Through a guard of honour of wee white antirrhinums.
I shake hands solemnly with Alan Breck Stewart,
Robert Bruce, Richard Coeur de Lion,
Robin Hood, Biggles, the crew of HMS Ulysses.
I bow low, then stride through the sandstone, whispering
Cambuslang, Cambuslang.

The Umbrella Stand

The eroticism of hand-knitted cardigans,
Shower caps and overshoes, wee earthenware pigs
Just to take the chill off the sheets

Dogs me: endearments of freely given
Potatoes and turnips, summer fruits,
Heinz 57, Milk Tray.

Sex was changing in a neuk in the rocks
Carefully into a one-piece bathing suit
On the edge of a cool, sunny ocean.

Sometimes at my parents' house I search
For that alert, tweed-flecky light in their eyes
Through which I came to exist.

The Numties

The parsnip Numties: I was a teenager then,
Collecting clip-together models
Of historical windsocks, dancing the Cumbernauld bump.

Satirical pornography, plant-staplers, nostalgiaform shoes
Were brochure-fresh. It was numty-four
I first saw a neighbour laughing in a herbal shirt.

Moshtensky, Garvin, Manda Sharry –
Names as quintessentially Numties
As Hearers and Bonders, duckponding, or getting a job

In eradication. Everything so familiar and sandwiched
Between the pre-Numties and the debouch of decades after.
I keep plunging down to the wreck

Of the submerged Numties, every year
Bringing back something jubilantly pristine,
Deeper drowned, clutching my breath.

Scotch Broth

A soup so thick you could shake its hand
And stroll with it before dinner.

The face rising to its surface,
A rayfish waiting to be stroked,

Is the pustular, eat-me face of a crofter,
Turnipocephalic, white-haired.

Accepting all comers, it's still our nation's
Flagsoup, sip-soup; sip, sip, sip

At this other scotch made with mutton
That intoxicates only

With peas and potatoes, chewy uists of meat.
All races breathe over our bowl,

Inhaling Inverness and Rutherglen,
Waiting for a big, teuchtery face

To compose itself from carrots and barley
Rising up towards the spoon.

Two-line Poem

On the centenary of the West Highland Line
for Wilson, Mary, and Joe

The first line starts with Glasgow, ends with Oban,
But the second breaks off, longer, more involved

With bog and dynamite. It sets down porters
At unmanned stations, returns to signalboxes

Sly engineers who built them, till it stops
With its origin – a low-paid army

Letting off steam: a lost legion of navvies
Pouring out their Roman aquaduct

At the head of Loch Shiel so we could sail along it
On rails that shone like water, speeding up

To our Railway Camping Coach at Morar station,
My father's hand trying not to break the mantle

When he lights the gas lamps and we go
To bed, three extra sleepers on that siding.

Past Polnish schoolhouse where the Rosses waved
Lochailort platform's rucksacked with our friends

Who picnic with us, pouring tomato soup
From a tartan flask. Some wear

The uniforms of the old North British Railway,
Others have Seventies sci-fi Nehru jackets

Or are unborn, but all are pulled by engines
Waiting at red lights to pass one another

On the single track. Today at Arisaig
An Edwardian telegraphist rattles down her window to speak,

Then the whistle goes and our two long trains snake out
In opposite directions – future, past –

But this evening and every other evening
These two will pass again, almost on time.

La Mer

Is that a bathing cap or a seal's head
Surfacing in the 1930s?

This morning the sea does a huge baking
Of scones and fresh apple tart,

Mixed up with herring, cod and shrimps,
Cuttlefish, fruits de mer.

The sea clears everything away
To set a fresh place. It repeats itself

Like Alzheimer's Disease.
Its moony rollers cast me ashore –

A creel, a fishbox from Crail or Vilnius,
A piece of boat, old but ready

To be put to some startling re-use.
Voices, phonelines, everything flows:

Dad in his landing-craft, beached
At Normandy, us cruising the Small Isles

In the Seventies, Eigg, Rhum, Muck, Canna
Bobbing up one by one, dark collies

Chasing their tails, retrieving sticks from the breakers,
Mr McConnochie's painting of Aphrodite

Breezing to the Arisaig beach on a clamshell.
When I was wee I knew the music

Was about the sea, but I thought its title
Was a French phrase meaning 'My Mother'.

Winter

That night we drove to hear about adoption
You jumped an unmarked junction, trying to find
The Social Work Centre. When we did, we sat
Ten minutes in the warm car, then went in.

We were the quietest of all the couples.
The walls were covered in felt-pen drawings, toys
Cluttered the place. Committedly,
A foster-parent told us what that meant

But cold seeped in from black-iced Dundee streets;
Swing-doors blew open; if it snowed, they'd close the bridge,
Stranding us there. I couldn't really tell
Just what we wanted. I wanted too much:

Not to feel so old, to be able to believe in luck,
To remember sitting with these other couples
In a semi-circle on bright scatter-cushions
Watching a vid in coats and anoraks.

Loganair

Below, a freelance palaeontologist
Gets stuck in with his JCB,

And here, from the winter airspace of Fife,
Coal-dark, nocturnal Burntisland

's drip-painted with streetlamps, the Forth's edge
Scribbled with motorway lights.

You're invisible. I'm fourteen thousand feet up,
Viewing the scan of our unborn child,

Nearing you over the prop-driven landscape,
Its November villages insect wings

Shimmering in carbon, carrying towards you
Cellophaned, machine-readable flowers.

Whisht

Wee towdy mowdy creel, peat wame,
Folic acid bank,
Ye ken the showers tae come, an ken
The pechin, pechin kink

O aa the born glens,
Corbetts an craigs, scamperin
Hutherons an fleckies, streakers, pods
The warld is mam tae, whan yi're great, then green.

Whisper

Little lovely womb, peaty womb, peat-bank of folic acid, you know the birthpangs to come, and know the panting, panting convulsive catching of the breath of all the born glens, mountains and crags, scampering young heifers and spotted cows, fast hunting dogs and neat small beasts that the world is midwife to, when you're big with child, then after the delivery.

The Handshakes

I flinched at the handshake of a woman in labour
Through mid-contraction when you pushed our son

Down towards the forceps.
Soon his fingers curled

Possessively around my index finger
And then round yours,

Welcoming us with a reflex action
To take your hand beyond yon Labour Suite

Where you clutched me as you breathed the Entonox
And called for your own mother, who is dead.

The Criticism

I who can't play any instrument,
Whose singing is crap, who was once chucked out of a choir

For my utterly expressionless face,
Sing to my baby till his rubbed-at eyelids

Waver. He sprawls in my arms
Not knowing if he's hearing 'The Skye Boat Song',

'Silent Night' or some early Seventies
TV soundtrack. He falls asleep

With a whole-body look of ecstatic boredom,
His breathing in tune with my own.

Kathleen Jamie

Permanent Cabaret

Our highwire artiste,
knowing nothing of fear, will take
sparkling risks fifty feet high.
Her costume, ladies, is iced with
hard diamonds.
While she mounts all those steps
our old friend the clown will stand
upside down in a shower of confetti
and chirp 'Love me!'

Their lamp is the last on camp to go out.
Coco reads Jung, sometimes aloud to
Estelle, if she's sewing on sequins.
More often she practises alone in the ring
for the day she enters permanent cabaret,
perhaps in Zurich. Coco cracks his knuckles,
thinking vaguely of children, or considers
repainting the outside of their van.

Half way across Estelle glitters like frost.
She has frozen. 'Remain professional.' She
draws breath through her teeth, wavers
her hand: 'Let Coco sense something for once!'
His red boots are edging towards her. He
coaxes, offers aid – his absurd umbrella.
The audience wonder: is it part of the show
this embarrassing wobbling,
this vain desperation to clutch?

Abir

There is the future Abir told me about
in the room where she showed me photographs
and served Turkish coffee.

She stared at the black grounds in my cup.
There was a slight smell of camphor. She
nodded and smiled. Apparently

I think too much, and will make journeys. Tomorrow
she'll make coffee, and curl her sisters' hair. She
asked me only the English for 'husband'.

This morning Abir will buy fruit in the market:
her cane chair creaks to itself in the heat. She'll
be home before the sun lies smashed on the streets.

Black Spiders

He looked up to the convent
she'd gone to. She answered no questions
but he knew by the way she'd turned away
that morning.
He felt like swimming to the caves.

*

The nuns have retreated. The eldest still
peals the bell in glee, although no one comes
from the ruins. All their praying was done
when they first saw the ships and the Turks'
swords reflecting the sun.

In the convent the cistern is dry,
the collection boxes empty – cleft skulls
severed and bleached,
are kept in a shrine, and stare to the East.

*

She caught sight of him later, below, brushing salt
from the hair of his nipples. She wanted them
to tickle; black spiders on her lips.

November

He can touch me with a look
as thoughtless as afternoon
and think as much of hindering me
as he would of sailing away.

In November, when the storms come
he drums his fingers on his books and turns
them into a fist that crashes. On the shore
where he insists we walk, he holds me like a man
at a deck-rail in a gale. I suspect his eyes
are open, red and gazing over my head
in the direction of abroad.

I am left to tell him in a voice that
seems as casual as his talk of travel:
I think as much of leaving as
of forcing him to stay.

The Barometer

Last year
Mother threw the barometer
the length of the corridor. This:
she has set her jaw. There's a chill
and the rustle of weeds. She's come in
from the garden, now she'll withdraw.

The maids are shivering. Outside
they're talking of snow. I say no
to a fire – it's an act of surrender.

I can see the bare fields from here
on the balcony. The nights
are growing longer. I know.
At least the harvest is gathered and safe.
– Every thanksgiving
I dance like a Romany. Indian summers;
I giggle and weep. Mother and me
go picnics in the blossoming . . .

My furs are laid out and waiting.
The maids keep tutting.
I catch myself biting
dead skin from my lips.
I have played with my gloves all day.

I ought just to jump
and meet Hades half way.

Inhumation

No one knows if he opened his eyes,
acknowledged the dark,
felt around, found and drank
the mead provided, supposing
himself dead.

from A FLAME IN YOUR HEART

What you said about being shot down –
I think I know (I shouldn't compare). At the bus stop
someone was reading the news. I strained
to see the list, you know, of names,
caught sight of what looked like 'Appleton'. The rain
came on, drops landing on the page
spread through. He folded it away
before I could see if it was true.

There was a sort of quiet feeling, as if
wardrobes and pianos were falling silently downstairs,
before the plummet, what happened you said
when you were hit, how the ground rears up like a rabid mare.
I couldn't stop falling down this spiral pit, expecting
to meet rock, or the sea. All the time I was changing sheets.
Jane was kind, though I didn't say. When she spoke,
it was like a wireless playing to an empty Mess.

It was four hours before I saw a paper. The name
was Applethwaite. Remember when you pushed
the stick into the hand of the blind man
who'd dropped it, and was panicky? I felt like him,
like you lads when you regain control,
lift the aircraft out of its spin, get the earth
beneath again. Len, I can't help but imagine
this crumpled shape: your plane; *Mrs* Applethwaite.

She scans the same horizon
from the other side
and I can almost touch her hands,
her kiss falls just too light.

Fräulein, one of us will burn tonight.
The other will waltz with an airman,
listen to the day's war news.
And I can almost reach her hands.

We don't have seasons, we just repeat
the same on a groaning train of men
who get discharged at the other end.
Under our hands, nothing changes.

I want to be a Land Girl with itching eyes,
I want you to see me rise from a wheat field,
stretch to ease an aching back, drive tractors
through orchards, let the sun slap me, sweat,
let the grime smeared on my brow run into furrows
that will turn into wrinkles one day. Not yet.
Let us girls throw our arms around each other's necks,
smell cattle and soil, give that direct
feminine leer to trucks passing full
of lewd soldiers. Let me cut down a harvest.
I want to take tea-breaks lying flat on my back,
to accept without question whatever pictures occur
in the clouds. Just let me get these
damned stockings off. I'd walk home at twilight,
cry with the cows if I wanted,
instead of holding it back.

Out in the fields is death at its best:
owls pick off the slowest mice, moles'
skin-and-bone dangle from fences. I want
growth: dirt on my delicate hands.

You'd think the simple pale blue page
a window, so clearly can I see through
to the Dispersal Hut. They were
fully kitted up. It's hot, they sweat,
Canadian Al plays cat's-cradle, hums,
two kip in chairs, there's
the occasional flick of a page
of 'Picture Post'. And Len, the one
who must keep busy, his
left hand's thrust knuckle deep in his hair.
He leans over the table, puts the date,
locks his ankles, writes 'Dear Katie',
and tells his news. Always in pencil –
the schoolboy, the apprentice
in his 'hell of a fellow' flying kit.
How the point wears down to dull
and flat, at the foot of the page,
where he says 'We've flown four sorties already today.'

If you knew that little force
when I press stamps, then unthinking
watch my letter fall into the box . . .

That gentle touch
I feel beneath my ears
as you raise my face to yours . . .

I still kiss you, though I know
that soft pressing of the thumb
is all it takes to kill a man.

Blood? Only port wine, suddenly drunk,
who's that giggling? Coughing on dust,
a stairway pointing up to the sky
naked and rude, terribly funny.

And a sharp tearing. I'm swearing,
there's fizzing and gurgling from severed
pipes, cuts on my legs, all the bells ringing
my head, here come people. Dust settles down
like a sigh. It all becomes clear.

Sharp as blades.
'I've torn my dress!' Laughing again.
The old barman who was chatting me up,
he's weeping over a stone. I mutter
'come now' so arch 'there's a war on, you know',

digging like a dog for a bone. Blue
to the lips, and I hear the word
he's about to utter, plea and command:
'Nurse?' Saw an arm. I thought:
'That's the last time I talk to strangers
in pubs. Should say I'm a typist.'

War Widow

You know I keep the photograph
beside my bed. It gathers glances
like I could
when I swayed my way amongst airmen.

The trees behind you are still
fresh, your face never changes.

My stocking seams aren't quite so straight.
My uniform's returned. You wear yours
somewhere,
caught in a snapshot while you slept.

Julian of Norwich

Everything I do I do for you.
Brute. You inform the dark
inside of stones, the winds draughting in

from this world and that to come,
but never touch me.
You took me on

but dart like a rabbit into holes
from the edges of my sense
when I turn, walk, turn.

*

I am the hermit whom you keep
at the garden's end, but I wander.
I am wandering in your acres

where every step, were I
attuned to sense them,
would crush a thousand flowers.

(Hush, that's not the attitude)
I keep prepared a room and no one comes.
(Love is the attitude)

*

Canary that I am, caged and hung
from the eaves of the world
to trill your praise.

He will not come.
Poor bloodless hands, unclasp.
Stiffened, stone-cold knees, bear me up.

(And yet, and yet, I am suspended
in his joy, huge and helpless
as the harvest moon in a summer sky.)

Peter the Rock

The last trumpet of sunlight blows over the sea.
He moves high on the cliff, sure of his grace
and raises an arm. The fingers connect.
He pulls up and leans out, hair falling straight toward earth.

He tells me he dreams about nothing
but falling, though we sleep on the sand.
His arms always round me, golden hair
spilled over my face. That mysterious injury
torn in his shoulders: 'I told you, I fell.'

Even in kissing you feel for holds,
grip through to bone.
It doesn't surprise me, I do it myself,
enrage you with symbol, the meaning of things.
You practise moves and hate gestures,
God-talk with vengeance, imperfect shoulders.

I change the tapes. He drives, and will go on denying
into the night. There is nothing
but rock and the climbing of rock under the sun.
Which I say is falling and setting behind us, unfolded,
flashed in the wing mirrors, golden, your skin tone.

Jane

'Would Miss Jane Eyre please report to Airport Information. Miss Jane Eyre, please.' – heard over PA at Heathrow

and he thrust himself into the streams
from every continent – a salmon
shouldering, winding,
searching for a face as pale as chalk.
A bookstore! Surely she'd be there,
peering at the print of worlds she recognized?
No. Nor in the transit lounge
with massive Asian families,
nor the Ladies, weeping beneath
the mounting roar of jets and air-conditioning.
He leaps the stairs – she may be taking
a demure, if plastic, cup of tea –
and surveys the concourse. A dark
hooded bird of prey, he sifts, sifts
the dress of all the nations
for a frock in English grey.
Would he catch her tiny voice
in this damned babble?
The information desk – she shakes her head.
'Shall I page again, sir?'
He gives a brusque 'No. It was an
off-chance, just an off-chance.'
'Is the lady departing or arriving, sir,
from where?' But he's striding
from the terminal, and minutes later,
his Land Rover nudges the northbound carriageway.

The Latter-day Noah

At last there's industry, heaven-sent work,
batter and clang from the shipyard.
Horses are snorting, pulling in wood, pitch,
hammers. Tell me, what is our cargo?
He nodded out of the window. 'Archetypes.'
And where do we take them? He went on staring.
'Just sail. And keep sailing. Sail over the
edge if you must.' We'll be killed! 'On the contrary
you might find an island.'
With the tigers and sharks?
'I'll send you a sign.' What'll that be?
'A rainbow.' Another arc? You're obsessed!
'You'll all live there forever.'
You mean frogs are immortal?
'The greenfly are . . . Forms. The cats are not
actual. You must sail to the heavens . . .' What?
'The transcendent.' But that isn't charted!
'True, but it's near and very like this,'
he said, reaching out to the window,
touching the rain through the glass.

The Philosopher Extemporizes in the Fairground

Should we accept the solar system
is, so, in fact, to speak
a Ferris wheel,

(albeit Royal, Televised, Electric and
Noted for Pleasing Young and Old
in Safety and Comfort)

and we are shackled by luck
into this turquoise cart
and here secured

by a tattooed gypsy who
sets the wheel rolling
only to leave

to watch his son walk the nebulous
waltzers, like some casual
Christ on water?

Then. He is neglecting us.
We are slowing down.
Our sky blue vehicle

may well attain that coveted
space, point the highest,
nearest the stars.

We may well sway above
the lurid art
and flashes

and little golden fishes.
Never, however, the less
we thinkers descend

and must assume we will meet
with no greater end than a jerk
of our tinker's thumb.

The Way We Live

Pass the tambourine, let me bash out praises
to the Lord God of movement, to Absolute
non-friction, flight, and the scarey side:
death by avalanche, birth by failed contraception.
Of chicken tandoori and reggae, loud, from tenements,
commitment, driving fast and unswerving
friendship. Of tee-shirts on pulleys, giros and Bombay,
barmen, dreaming waitresses with many fake-gold
bangles. Of airports, impulse, and waking to uncertainty,
to strip-lights, motorways, or that pantheon –
the mountains. To overdrafts and grafting

and the fit slow pulse of wipers as you're
creeping over Rannoch, while the God of moorland
walks abroad with his entourage of freezing fog,
his bodyguard of snow.
Of endless gloaming in the North, of Asiatic swelter,
to launderettes, anecdotes, passions and exhaustion,
Final Demands and dead men, the skeletal grip
of government. To misery and elation; mixed,
the sod and caprice of landlords.
To the way it fits, the way it is, the way it seems
to be: let me bash out praises – pass the tambourine.

from KARAKORAM HIGHWAY

The wave breaks on the smallest stone,
rolls on. Dawn as eternal occurrence;
always some place. Darkness, dusk, day,
seem immutable as the poplar trees
that make a place. It's permanent
midnight at that check-point, or where
the herd and goats turned to stare
forever half-light, soft as chicks.
Unmanned border of night and day, we rumble on
toward the sun – a tiny cut in orange peel,
sharp sting of smell – Ah, breakfast!

At the sharp end of the gorge;
the bridge. Like a single written word
on vast and rumpled parchment. Bridge.
The statement of man in landscape.

And how they guard it.
Drifts of people on either bank
like brackets, knowing it can crash
to the river in a mangled scribble
and be erased.
They write it up again, single syllable
of construction
shouted over the canyon.

And all the driver wants is eye-drops
before he straightens up the bus, commits us.
At least malevolence concedes your existence;
worse is indifference, power and indifference.
The river brawls beneath us, self-obsessed,
narcissistic. Wheels turn, turn again, full weight.
The bridge starts to undulate and we're hanging
out of windows half-roads over the Indus,
grinning at each other, impotent, enlightened.
The world grew tight.

It must have been about then we first saw the mountains.

It's earthly and brown, deep inside canyons.
Stones at the roadside:
'Here rock fell on men', 'men fell to the river'
and the river and rock were unmoved
being river and rock.
He takes it fast.
Some nameless white mountain
has closed off the end of the canyon.
The walls grow taller, the river hysterical.
He brakes, hauls the wheel. No talking.
No colour but brown –
except in the mind. It's been many hours.
Fear passes out into long passive blue,
a slight smile – there is nothing at all we can do.
And the sky widens, the canyon gives out
to a strange sort of kingdom
and the first hanging village swings in.

The year's greening crop spilled
down dull unaltering rock like the tail
of a bird. We can recognize this:

that crops yellow, get cut,
turn in on themselves over winter, head under wing,
and begin to feel like ourselves again.

Suspended villages, terraces
layered wide in the movement of scythes,
the unthreatening gesture of sowing.

That day was raised, a song of a note
from the clapped-out engine. Headwind, hot
in our eyes. Streams, children
splashing down to the roadside, wave,
flowers jammed into their hands 'K2 going?' and
the corn is yellow banked up the hillside.
Lost in dust. This jeep-ride takes us to mountains.

Maybe I'm drowning and this is my life: flashes
on birds' wings, head shaking delight,
beasts in the shade, greenery, embroidery,
women in shawls with the same limbless sway
as a poplar. Grubby babies on roofs, goats,
yaks in a farmyard. Here and passed.
Tree-tips high against blue.
Berries fell to our laps – is this Eden? –
we ate them. Mohammed Ali threw his hat,
caught it, laughed, and
an old dame up an apricot tree
surveyed her river, her valley. High state
of movement, track climbing to meet us
appearing, like everything else at a distance
to blend into heat, to shimmer like mercury.
The shimmer of joy on the face of uncertainty.

from THE AUTONOMOUS REGION

O a great downward lurch of the heart, as though
he dreamily stepped off an unexpected kerb;
Fa-hsien in the city. He says:
 '*Need all situations be resolvable/resolved?*'
or
 '*Is* there a high pass over the mountains?'

and hopes/hopes not. Rumour flits the city
like bats, flits the city like bats by night,
rumours on the lips of running tea-boys,
delivered on the hour, on trays like tea.
 And the rumours say yes, the rumours say no.

And with a great shout and a creak
the shoulders of 100 youths
pulled the wingèd city gates, and all
that were going walked or rode
out to the desert before them.

Fires burning in the bellies of yurts at the day's end:
beside a river, such a clear stream there, with a fish.
If he could return he'd return to that river
as the sun rose like a fish behind mountains
and the stream, cleared to crystal foretold.
A purple range to East and to West,
he remarks:

'Not a few have turned back.
Promise or rumour without author or source
ever keeps us moving, against the way
of the small clear river' – which is to say: uphill.
Devotions over, the ice mountains'
jagged edges met his gaze. He smiles, 'Life!
Wo! *That* straggling caravan.' Then: 'But what to you
are the ramblings of Fa-hsien?' Begins to walk.

Walked beneath the power lines
(sagging like pigs' bellies in the sun)
between the desert graves and gravel mounds,
scared the crows with open black beaks, walked
abandoned tar-barrels, wiped the sweat
and wondered aloud:

'How did this begin?'

just one tiny act: he'd dropped the keys back
thro' the letter-box.
And though molten tar got stuck to his feet,
all in all he thought it rather wonderful.
He said to himself:

'Well, is there?'

when, to others insisted:

'There *is*.' Secretly, he loved

the way his lips cracked, loved
to feel his head spin, loved
to cough the dust and consider himself
a journeyman, a-journeying.

Carved dragons framed the door, fierce and delicate
our house-on-stilts. Creepers chased like monkeys
round our high, half-hidden walls whose gates
opened onto tree-tops; streams
flashing to the village pleased us first. I loved
the tremors that occasionally bucked
our youthful gorge as if a finger
traced its spine. My colour then
was mother-of-pearl; my bed and bedding,
nails, the combs that held my ornate hair . . .
I'd lean on the verandah, breathe jasmine
air, lean on the verandah, lean and fancy.
But I loved it best when snow came, the distant world
would soothe its troubled self into a pearl.

The Travels of Fa-hsien

His bed is hard, his smell
a travel-musk of months through teeming villages.
The walls of course are stained, the sheet
he almost envies: old, plain.

He rises, ties his top-knot, wanders
to the boiler-room, with his
double-happiness thermos flask,
noting
          every vessel can be broken, filled,
and he is empty, these days. Not old
as the sun-lines round his eyes suggest
which eyes have seen:
                    many things out of strong places
et cetera. And who knows what his robe conceals:
tattoos, a bleeding heart.

*

There's roads and there are one-horse-towns
and any climb out of hamlet, gorge or wilderness
he looks in wonder,
to fellow travellers he replies:
'What wisdom have I gathered? None!
That's my tuppence worth', walks on.
'Threw it in a ditch and walk unburdened.'

And also in the ditch, a dog, days dead, ignored.
'I've lied and vowed at umpteen altars,
and know I can be
                              utterly deceived.
Perhaps still am.'

At the thin black line of shade at a truckstop
while they fix the fan-belt
and there's no water
he'll bring out yarrow-stalks, divine.
And sometimes, walking alone, he finds
the centre of his being, flinches,
for it's nowt
                    but an alms bowl.
Waiting at a roadside, he scratches the dust
with a stick, finds: more dust.
In the hot shade of some godforsaken Xinjiang bunkhouse
remembers the river and the fish.

(o monk, whither do you wander?
to garner wisdom and bring scripture home)

Xiahe

Abune the toon o Xiahe
a thrast monstery,
warn lik a yowe's tuith.

The sun gawps at innermaist
ingles o wa's.
Secret as speeders

folk hae criss-crosst a saucht
seedit i the yird flair
wi rags o win blawn prayer.

Xiahe. Wave droonin wave
on a pebbly shore,
the *ahe* o machair, o slammach,

o impatience; ahent the saft saltire
i trashed, an sheep;
wha's drift on the brae

is a lang cloud's shadda.
The herd cries a wheen wirds
o Tibetan sang,

an A'm waukenet, on a suddenty mindit:
A'm far fae hame,
I hae crossed China.

Xiahe (pronounced *Shi-ah-e*): a Tibetan town in the now Chinese province of Gansu; **sauch**: willow; **yird**: earth; **slammach**: cobweb.

The Queen of Sheba

Scotland, you have invoked her name
just once too often
in your Presbyterian living rooms.
She's heard, yea
even unto heathenish Arabia
your vixen's bark of poverty, come down
the family like a lang neb, a thrawn streak,
a wally dug you never liked
but can't get shot of.

She's had enough. She's come.
Whit, tae this dump? Yes!
She rides first camel
of a swaying caravan
from her desert sands
to the peat and bracken
of the Pentland hills
across the fit-ba pitch
to the thin mirage
of the swings and chute; scattered with glass.

Breathe that steamy musk
on the Curriehill Road, not mutton-shanks
boiled for broth, nor the chlorine stink
of the swimming pool where skinny girls
accuse each other of verrucas.
In her bathhouses women bear
warm pot-bellied terracotta pitchers
on their laughing hips.
All that she desires, whatever she asks

She will make the bottled dreams
of your wee lasses
look like *sweeties.*

Spangles scarcely cover
her gorgeous breasts, hanging gardens
jewels, frankincense; more voluptuous
even than Vi-next-door, whose
high-heeled slippers
keeked from dressing gowns
like little hooves, wee tails
of pink fur stuffed in the cleavage of her toes;
more audacious even than Currie Liz
who led the gala floats
through the Wimpey scheme
in a ruby-red Lotus Elan
before the Boys' Brigade band
and the Brownies' borrowed coal-truck;
hair piled like candy-floss;
who lifted her hands fom the neat wheel
to tinkle her fingers
at her tricks
among the Masons and the elders and the police.

The cool black skin
of the Bible couldn't hold her,
nor the atlas green
on the kitchen table,
you stuck with thumbs
and split to fruity hemispheres
yellow Yemen, Red Sea, *Ethiopia.* Stick in
with the homework and you'll be
cliver like yer faither.
but no too cliver,
no *above yersel.*

See her lead those great soft camels
widdershins round the kirk-yaird,
smiling
as she eats
avocados with apostle spoons
she'll teach us how. But first

she wants to strip the willow
she desires the keys
        to the National Library
she is beckoning
    the lasses
    in the awestruck crowd . . .

Yes, we'd like to
        clap the camels,
to smell the spice,
admire her hairy legs and
bonny wicked smile, we want to take
PhDs in Persian, be vice
to her president: we want
to help her
    ask some Difficult Questions

she's shouting for our wisest man
to test her mettle:

    Scour Scotland for a Solomon!

Sure enough: from the back of the crowd
someone growls:
                whae do you think y'ur?

and a thousand laughing girls and she
draw our hot breath
        and shout:
THE QUEEN OF SHEBA!

Hand Relief

Whatever happened to friends like Liz,
who curled her legs on a leather settee,
and touched your knee, girl/girl,
as she whispered what the businessmen of Edinburgh
wear beneath their suits –

laughed and hooked her hair back
saying Tuesday, giving some bloke
hand relief, she'd looked up at the ceiling
for the hundredth time that lunch-hour,
and screaming, slammed the other hand down hard
on the panic button; had to stand there
topless in front of the bouncers
and the furious punter, saying
sorry, I'm sorry, it was just a spider . . .

Whatever happens to girls like Liz
fresh out of school, at noon on a Saturday
waiting for her shift at Hotspots
sauna, in a dressing gown
with a pink printed bunny
who follows you to the window
as you look out at the city
and calls you her pal. She says, *you're a real pal.*

Child with Pillar-box and Bin-bags

But it was the shadowed street-side she chose
while Victor Gold the bookies basked
in conquered sunlight, and though
Dalry Road Licensed Grocer gloried and cast
fascinating shadows she chose
the side dark in the shade of tenements;
that corner where Universal Stores' (closed
for modernization) blank hoarding blocked
her view as if that process were illegal;
she chose to photograph her baby here,
the corner with the pillar-box.
In his buggy, which she swung to face her.
She took four steps back, but
the baby in his buggy rolled toward the kerb.
She crossed the ground in no time
it was fearful as Niagara,
she ran to put the brake on, and returned
to lift the camera, a cheap one.
The tenements of Caledonian Place neither
watched nor looked away, they are friendly buildings.
The traffic ground, the buildings shook, the baby breathed
and maybe gurgled at his mother as she
smiled to make him smile in his picture;
which she took on the kerb in the shadowed corner,
beside the post-box, under tenements, before
the bin-bags hot in the sun that shone
on them, on dogs, on people on the other side
the other side of the street to that she'd chosen,
if she'd chosen or thought it possible to choose.

Wee Wifey

I have a demon and her name is
WEE WIFEY
I caught her in a demon trap – the household of my skull
I pinched her by her heel throughout her wily transformations
until
she confessed
her name indeed to be WEE WIFEY
and she was out to do me ill.

So I made great gestures like Jehovah: dividing
land from sea, sea from sky,
my own self from WEE WIFEY
(*There*, she says, *that's tidy!*)

Now I watch her like a dolly
keep an eye,
and mourn her:
For she and I are angry/cry
because we love each other dearly.
It's sad to note
that without
WEE WIFEY
I shall live long and lonely as a tossing cork.

Perfect Day

I am just a woman of the shore
wearing your coat against the snow
that falls on the oyster-catchers' tracks
and on our own; falls
on the still grey waters
of Loch Morar, and on our shoulders
gentle as restraint: a perfect weight
of snow as tree-boughs
and fences bear against a loaded sky:
one flake more, they'd break.

Mr and Mrs Scotland are Dead

On the civic amenity landfill site,
the coup, the dump beyond the cemetery
and the 30-mile-an-hour sign, her stiff
old ladies' bags, open mouthed, spew
postcards sent from small Scots towns
in 1960: Peebles, Largs, the rock-gardens
of Carnoustie, tinted in the dirt.
Mr and Mrs Scotland, here is the hand you were dealt:
fair but cool, showery but nevertheless,
Jean asks kindly; the lovely scenery;
in careful school-room script –
The Beltane Queen was crowned today.
But Mr and Mrs Scotland are dead.

Couldn't he have burned them? Released
in a grey curl of smoke
this pattern for a cable knit? Or this:
tossed between a toppled fridge
and sweet-stinking anorak: *Dictionary for Mothers*
M: – Milk, *the woman who worries . . .*;
And here, Mr Scotland's John Bull Puncture Repair Kit;
those days when he knew intimately
the thin roads of his country, hedgerows
hanged with small black brambles' hearts;
and here, for God's sake, his last few joiners' tools,
SCOTLAND, SCOTLAND, stamped on their tired handles.

Do we take them? Before the bulldozer comes
to make more room, to shove aside
his shaving brush, her button tin.

Do we save this toolbox, these old-fashioned views
addressed, after all, to Mr and Mrs Scotland?
Should we reach and take them? And then?
Forget them, till that person enters
our silent house, begins to open
to the light our kitchen drawers,
and performs for us this perfunctory rite:
the sweeping up, the turning out.

Arraheids

See thon raws o flint arraheids
in oor gret museums o antiquities
awful grand in Embro –
Dae'ye near'n daur wunner at wur histrie?
Weel then, Bewaur!
The museums of Scotland are wrang.
They urnae arraheids
but a show o grannies' tongues,
the hard tongues o grannies
aa deid an gaun
back to thur peat and burns,
but for thur sherp
chert tongues, that lee
fur generations in the land
like wicked cherms, that lee
aa douce in the glessy cases in the gloom
o oor museums, an
they arenae lettin oan. But if you daur
sorn aboot an fancy
the vanished hunter, the wise deer runnin on;
wheesht . . . an you'll hear them,
fur they cannae keep fae muttering
ye arenae here tae wonder,
whae dae ye think ye ur?

Rooms

Though I love this travelling life and yearn
like ships docked, I long
for rooms to open with my bare hands,
and there discover the wonderful, say
a ship's prow rearing, and a ladder
of rope thrown down.
Though young, I'm weary:
I'm all rooms at present, all doors
fastened against me;
but once admitted start craving
and swell for a fine, listing ocean-going prow
no man in creation can build me.

Skeins o Geese

Skeins o geese write a word
across the sky. A word
struck lik a gong
afore I wis born.
The sky moves like cattle, lowin.

I'm as empty as stane, as fields
ploo'd but not sown, naked
an blin as a stane. Blin
tae the word, blin
tae a' soon but geese ca'ing.

Wire twists lik archaic script
roon a gate. The barbs
sign tae the wind as though
it was deef. The word whustles
ower high for ma senses. Awa.

No lik the past which lies
strewn aroun. Nor sudden death.
No like a lover we'll ken
an connect wi forever.
The hem of its goin drags across the sky.

Whit dae birds write on the dusk?
A word niver spoken or read.
The skeins turn hame,
on the wind's dumb moan, a soun,
maybe human, bereft.

The Tay Moses

What can I fashion
for you but a woven
creel of river-
rashes, a golden
oriole's nest, my gift
wrought from the Firth –

and choose my tide; either
the flow, when water-tight,
you'll drift to the uplands –
my favourite hills; held
safe in eddies, where salmon,
wisdom and guts
withered in spawn,
rest between moves: that
slither of body as you were born;

or the ebb, when the water
will birl you to snag
on reeds, the river-
pilot leaning over the side:
'*Name o God!*' and you'll change hands
tractor-man, grieve,
to the farm-wife, who
takes you into her
competent arms

even as I drive, slamming
the car's gears;
spitting gravel on tracks
down between berry-fields,
engine still racing, the door wide,
as I run toward her, crying
LEAVE HIM! Please,
it's okay, he's mine.

Crossing the Loch

Remember how we rowed toward the cottage
on the sickle-shaped bay,
that one night after the pub
loosed us through its swinging doors,
and we pushed across the shingle, till
water lipped the sides
as though the loch mouthed 'boat'?
City kids,
a distant yellow glow was Glasgow.

I forget who rowed. Our jokes hushed
to the oars' splash, creak, and the spill
of the loch reached long into the night.
Out in the race I was scared:
the cold shawl of breeze
and hunched hills; what the water held
of deadheads, ticking nuclear hulls.

Who rowed, and who kept their peace,
who hauled salt air and stars
deep into their lungs, were not reassured;
and who first cried the dim glitter
of the loch's phosphorescence;
so now, like a twittering nest
washed from the rushes, an astonished
small boat of saints,
we watched water shine on our fingers and oars;
the magic dart of our bow-wave.

It was surely fool-hardy, such a broad loch, a tide

but we live, and even have children
to women and men we had yet to meet
that night we set out, calling our own
the sky and salt water, wounded hills
dark-starred by blae-berries, the glimmering anklets
we wore in the shallows
as we shipped oars and jumped,
to draw the boat safe, high at the cottage shore.

Song of Sunday

A driech day, and nothing to do
bar watch starlings flichter
over soup-bones
left on a plate on the grass.
All forenoon broth-barley, marrowfat peas
swelled in a kitchen jug,
and I soaked stamps, corners
torn from polite white envelopes
in a saucer till they
peeled clear, neither soggy
nor still stuck, 'see, watch and not
tear them – wait at peace'.

There'd aye be women
in the kitchen, brisket
lashed in string, tatties
peeled lovelessly, blinded
pale and drowned. See if one
now nicked herself
with a paring-knife
and spell-bound, the house
froze still warm to the touch,
till hacking back in
through privet and rowan
past the starlings' diorama
toward my father caught
mid stretch-and-yawn,
wee sister playing Sindys
with the girl next door; now

I could wake you
with something alien
and lovely
as a kiss . . .

and we'd be called to eat
what's put in front of us: potatoes, meat,
till we could get down *Please*.
There were African leopards on TV,
and Songs of Praise. My stamps were dry
the odd USA, Magyar Poste exotic
among the tuppenny-ha'penny pinks
the wee lion
rampant in a corner,
and after homework I'd have time
to turn to 'Great Britain'
like I'd been shown,
fold and align the edges
with officious squares.
Press. 'Bedtime!' *There*.

Forget It

History in a new scheme. I strain
through hip, ribs, oxter, bursting
the cuff of my school-shirt, because
this, Mr Hannay, is me. *Sir!*
Sir!   *Sir!*
– he turns and I deflate and claim
just one of these stories,
razed places,
important as castles
as our own. *Mum!*

We done the slums today!
I bawled from the glass
front door she'd long desired.
What for? bangs the oven shut.
Some history's better forgot.
                    So how come
we remember the years
before we were born? Gutters
still pocked with 50s rain,
trams cruised dim
streetlit afternoons; war
at our backs. The black door
of the close wheezed
till you turned the third stair
then resounded like cannon.
A tower of banisters. Nana
and me toiled past windows
smeared in black-out, condemned
empty stone. The neighbours had flit
to council-schemes, or disappeared . . .

Who were the disappeared? Whose
the cut-throat
razor on the mantelpiece, what man's
coat hung thick with town-gas,
coal, in the lobby press?
And I mind
being stood, washed like a dog
with kettle and one cold tap
in a sink plumbed sheer
from the window
to the back midden
as multi-storeys rose
across the goods-yard,
and shunters clanked
through nights shared
in the kitchen recess bed.

I dreamed about my sister in America,
I doot she's dead. What rural
feyness this? Another sibling
lost in Atlantic cloud,
a hint of sea in the rain –
the married in England,
the drunken and the mad,
a couple of notes postmarked Canada,
then mist: but this is a past
not yet done; else how come
our parents slam shut; deny
like criminals: *I can't remember, cannae*
mind, then turn at bay: *Why?*

who wants to know? stories
spoken through the mouths
of closes; who cares
who trudged those worn stairs,

or daily ran down the very helix
of her genes, to play
in now rubbled back greens?
What happened about my grandad? Why
did Agnes go? How come
you don't know

that stories are balm,
ease their own pain, contain
a beginning, a middle –
and ours is a long driech
now demolished street. *Forget it!*
Forget them that vanished,
voted with their feet,
away for good
or ill through the black door
even before the great clearance came,
turning tenements outside-in,
exposing gas-pipes, hearths
in damaged gables, wallpaper
hanging limp and stained
in the shaming rain.

History, Mr Hannay.
The garden shrank for winter
and Mum stirred our spaghetti hoops
not long before she started back
part-time at Debenham's
to save for Christmas,
the odd wee
luxury, our first
foreign
holiday.

The Bogie-wife

She hoists her thigh over back fences,
not down the street, her feet squash
worms, hands stained brown as dung.

She flusters hens, looking for babies:
one eye swivelling in the middle of her forehead.
She leaves, like a yeti
the proof of her footprint.

Traffic on the road ignores her
the daylight is both broad and long;
our nouveaux arrivistes; businessmen, journalists,
know her for a daft village story, like the Black Beast.

She's simple, gets tangled in the netting
of raspberry-groves; but canny: keeps
to the railway wall, compost heaps.

She can smell babies, will push
between laundry hung to dry,
arms, strong as plum-boughs
twisting into fruit.

It's just her nature, she means no harm,
but the old wives run her out of town,
some banging pot-lids as others shout
This is Private Property! Ye've nae right!

But she is charming when cornered,
speaks a nice Scots,
wears a fresh tee-shirt and attractive batik trousers.

Acknowledgements

The poems in this selection are taken from the following books, to whose publishers acknowledgement is made: *Common Knowledge* (Secker & Warburg, 1991), *Feast Days* (Secker & Warburg, 1992), *The Myth of the Twin* (Jonathan Cape, 1994) and *Swimming in the Flood* (Jonathan Cape, 1995) for John Burnside; *A Scottish Assembly* (Chatto & Windus, 1990), *Sharawaggi* (with W. N. Herbert; Polygon, 1990), *Talkies* (Chatto & Windus, 1992) and *Masculinity* (Jonathan Cape, 1996) for Robert Crawford; *Black Spiders* (Salamander, 1982), *A Flame in Your Heart* (Bloodaxe, 1986), *The Way We Live* (Bloodaxe, 1987), *The Autonomous Region: Poems and Photographs from Tibet* (with Sean Smith; Bloodaxe, 1993) and *The Queen of Sheba* (Bloodaxe, 1994) for Kathleen Jamie.

The Graduates

If I chose children they'd know
stories of the old country, the place
we never left. I swear

I remember no ship
slipping from the dock,
no cluster of hurt, proud family,

waving till they were wee
as china milkmaids
on a mantelpiece,

but we have surely gone,
and must knock with brass
kilted pipers

doors to the old land;
we emigrants of no farewell
who keep our bit language

in jokes and quotes;
our working knowledge
of coal-pits, fevers: lost

like the silver bangle I lost
at the shows one Saturday
tried to conceal, denied

but they're not daft;
and my bright, monoglot bairns
will discover, misplaced

among the book-shelves,
proof, rolled in a red tube:
my degrees, a furled sail, my visa.